The First
Girl Guide

The First Girl Guide

The Story of Agnes Baden-Powell

Helen D. Gardner

AMBERLEY

This book is dedicated to all those who have shared with me a
Guiding adventure of over sixty years

First published 2010

Amberley Publishing Plc
Cirencester Road, Chalford,
Stroud, Gloucestershire, GL6 8PE

www.amberleybooks.com

British Library Cataloguing in Publication Data.
A catalogue record for this book is available
the British Library.

ISBN 978 1 4456 0010 9

Typesetting and Origination by Fonthill
Printed in Great Britain

Contents

Foreword

By
The Hon. Michael Baden-Powell

I am delighted this book has been written; I hope it will once and for all set the record straight in terms of how the Girl Guide Movement was established.

Agnes Baden-Powell was indeed a remarkable woman who must not be forgotten and with her brother, deserves recognition for creating the world's greatest Movement for women, the Girl Guides. Be as it may, it cannot be denied that my Grandmother Olave, played a vital role in the Guide Movement's continued development at a critical time, when the then fledgling Movement appeared to be faltering from within. It was Olave's youthful zest for challenge, her enormous sense of energy, her total belief in the principles of the Guide Law and the Promise she made at her investiture to carry through with those principles that finally enabled the establishment of the Movement to succeed. In this sense, both Agnes and Olave complemented each other's enormous sense of foresight and belief in the rights of women. There can be no doubt as a devoted sister and beloved wife of the Founder, each of these ladies made a significant contribution in establishing the World Girl Guide and Girl Scout Movement (WAGGGS).

Agnes was indeed an unusual person considering her background, born at a time when social attitudes towards women and what was expected were very different to modern times. A young woman in those times was presented at Court, traditionally became accomplished in such pursuits as sewing, poetry sessions, playing some musical instrument, dancing or looking after elderly family; a very different lifestyle to this day and age.

Agnes was the daughter of a University Professor-cum-clergyman who died whilst she was very young, and as the only daughter, she played out the role as a 'dutiful' daughter by living in her mother's shadow right up to the time of her mother's death. Sadly as a result, Agnes never married even though a number of opportunities existed.

Because money was always a problem for the family, Agnes had little formal education, yet she developed an inquiring mind and thanks to her younger brother Baden, she became interested in 'unlady like' activities such as shooting, fishing, sailing and camping with her brothers, bee keeping, rearing birds and especially flying, to the point of expressing a wish after the cessation of hostilities of the Second World War to learn to fly this new flying contraption called a helicopter; she was then 80 plus years of age. Because of her interest in flight, Agnes was for some years the only female member of the Royal Aeronautical Society and once held the air height flight record because of her ballooning experiences thanks to her brother Baden.

She developed an interest in an invention called radio and became friendly with Marconi, the man who invented radio. We believe Agnes may have taken an active part in some of Marconi's early experiments.

In spite of her busy lifestyle she still found time to write and publish the first handbook for the Girl Guides, *How Girls can help build up the Empire.*

I take this opportunity to congratulate Helen Gardner for taking the initiative to research and record this hitherto untold and wonderful unknown story of Agnes Baden-Powell, a remarkable woman to whom we owe a great debt of gratitude.

'She was indeed a woman of her time and before her time'. I hope you will enjoy reading this previously untold story as I did.

Acknowledgements

My thanks are due to many people. First, albeit belatedly, to the late Elaine Clark-Taylor. It was she who gave me the facsimile copy of 'How Girls Can Help . . .' which started me off on my journey, and who gave me so much affectionate support until her untimely death. And then my thanks go to Professor Dame Margaret Taylor-Warwick, Agnes' great-niece and the holder of many of the primary source papers which I have researched. She has opened her home to me in the most generous way and has been unstinting in her support. Other members of the Baden-Powell family have been of great help to me: the late the Hon. Betty Clay CBE, Lord Baden-Powell's daughter, who allowed me to do my initial research in her home; the late Francis Baden-Powell, the family Archivist, who was so helpful to me in the early days, and his widow, Cherry, who opened her home to me so that I could follow up on that work; the Hon. Michael Baden-Powell generously offered to write the Foreword and for this recognition I am grateful; Margaret Courteney, lately Archivist at Guide Headquarters, has been of enormous help and encouragement. Many members of the Trefoil Guild, and especially their archivists, including Susan Leng of Essex North East, have been very supportive. Lastly, and by no means least, I must thank my good friend Sally Phillips who has encouraged and advised me during the latter years of the work and who has compiled the index.

Prologue –
The Challenge of Agnes

Why should this book be written?

Most people, including those in Guiding, believe that Olave Baden-Powell started the Girl Guides. When I say that I am writing about Agnes they tell me they met her in 1953 or ... and I have to explain that it cannot have been Agnes as she died in 1945. So who was Agnes?

When Robert Baden-Powell, the hero of Mafeking, found himself inspecting a troop of 'Girl Scouts' at the Crystal Palace Rally in 1909, he had not even met his young future wife, Olave St Clair Soames. It was to his sister Agnes, his next in age and great friend, that he turned. It was Agnes who helped Robert to start the Girl Guides. A Victorian woman in every sense of the word, a woman in her fifties, yet she embarked on supporting her brother in his great project.

So what was it that made this woman tick? What was there in her Victorian upbringing that fitted her to help her brother with his revolutionary ideas for the training of young people? It is the hope of the writer that, through this book, we will find out who Agnes was, how her background had equipped her for leading the great game of Guiding, and how she was able to adapt and copy Scouting for the girls of her day.

There had, of course, been a copy in our Guide cupboard of *How Girls Can Help to Build up the Empire*, but I had never read it straight through. In 1992 I was given a copy of the newly published facsimile edition of this handbook and I became intrigued; Agnes, when she embarked on her great project, was about the same age that I was at the time, and I knew that I would not have had the necessary energy. Subsequently I heard a couple of anecdotes that concerned me. The first was a story of an experienced Guider who was showing a visitor round one of the Guide training centres, explaining how Olave had started the Girl Guides. The second incident was when the Guide Heritage Centre had opened at Headquarters and Betty Clay, the Founder's daughter who was being shown round, had pointed out that Agnes, like her brother, had red and not brown hair.

The time had come to write a book.

PART I

A Member of the Family

FAMILY LIFE

When Agnes was born into the Powell family on 16 December 1858 it might have been expected that the event would cause little excitement. She was, after all, her mother Henrietta's ninth child and her father Baden's thirteenth. But the Powell family liked their children and each new arrival was welcomed with excitement. Moreover Agnes, being a girl, brought special joy as the previous two daughters of the union had died in infancy. There would be only one more child after her. It seems that the eldest and youngest children remained at home for the birth, while the middle boys of the family stayed with their grandparents.

Agnes' father, Baden, was the son of a Kentish squire who had been High Sheriff of Kent and Master of the Mercers' Company. This last was a family tradition going back at least two hundred years and continues to the present day. His family had originated in the Mildenhall area of Suffolk, and moved to the City of London in the eighteenth century, before eventually moving out to Kent. At the age of seventeen Baden went up to Balliol College, Oxford, where he had a successful career, taking a First Class Degree in Mathematics in 1817, followed by his MA in 1820. The following year he was ordained into the Church of England and, after a short curacy at Midhurst in Kent, accepted the appointment of Vicar in Plumstead where he was to stay for six years. At about the same time that he moved to Plumstead, he married Eliza Rivaz who came from Hackney. As her name suggests, she had Italian relations and they would continue to play a significant part in the life of the family. There were no children of this marriage and Eliza died in 1836.

Eighteen months after the death of Eliza, Baden remarried, this time to Charlotte Pope who came from Middlesex. She would present her husband with four children: Charlotte Elizabeth was born on 14 September 1838, Baden Henry was born on 23 August 1841, Louisa Anne was born on 18 March 1843 and Laetitia Mary was born on 4 June 1844. The giving of the name Baden to the boy meant that, within twenty years, the family was to have the anomaly of two living sons who bore the same name. However, Baden Henry was destined to be a lawyer and to serve in India, which might have been expected to lessen any confusion. Charlotte died on 14 October 1844, leaving her husband with four children whose ages ranged from six years to six months.

By this time Baden was no longer working as a parish priest. His mathematical ability had always been outstanding and, in 1827, at the age of thirty-one, he had accepted the post of Savilian Professor of Geometry at Oxford where he had set up the family home in College Lane. One of his more notable actions in the early days of this appointment was when, in 1834, he was among the 'Noetics' who had the courage to vote for the admission of Dissenters (those who were not members of the Church of England) to the University.

Baden did not remain single for long. On his frequent visits to London he would often visit his old friend, Vice-Admiral Smyth, with whom he shared an interest in science and, in particular, astronomy. Vice-Admiral Smyth was a Fellow of the Royal Society, and his son, Piazzi, would become Astronomer Royal for Scotland. Young Henrietta Grace Smyth had long admired Professor Powell from her schoolroom; now she emerged into the world and loved to discuss science and astronomy with Baden. A deep relationship developed but Baden had reservations; after all, he was forty-nine and Henrietta was only twenty-two. Scruples were obviously overcome for they were married on 10 March 1846 at St Luke's Church in Chelsea and Henrietta was installed as the mistress of her husband's home in Oxford.

The Savilian Professor's young wife seems to have been quite a shock to Baden's University friends. She obviously introduced items of furniture in her own taste, for it was reported that she had furnished her drawing room with the new and highly fashionable spider-leg chairs. On one occasion, a large colleague of Baden's, by the name of Whately, was visiting. It is said that he sat, swinging, plunging and shifting as he talked, until an ominous crack was heard as a chair leg gave way whereon, without any comment, he tossed it on the sofa and moved to another chair.

It would seem that there was no intention of Henrietta becoming a mother to Baden's children. Very quickly they were shipped off to the various maternal relations who would be responsible for their upbringing. At least one of the girls made her home in Lisbon and it was from there that her son wrote in 1902 to tell Agnes that he had become engaged, so it is evident that contact was maintained.

When the first child arrived in February 1847 it was a boy, and he was baptised Henry Warington Smyth. He was followed in December of the same year by George Smyth. It becomes apparent that the names of all the children were to incorporate their mother's surname. There was a slightly longer pause before Augustus Smyth joined the family in May 1849, and then Francis Smyth in July 1850.

But the easy times were over and disaster began to hit the family. In October 1851 Henrietta Smyth was born, and then John Penrose Smyth in December 1852. However, in the following March, Henrietta died. Unusually for the Powells there was then quite a long gap. May there perhaps have been a miscarriage? Jessie Smyth was born in November 1855, before disaster struck again with the death, three weeks later, of John. Sorrow hit the family again with the death of Jessie in the following July. Thus, in the course of five years, Baden and his young wife had had, and lost, three of their children.

Such a bleak period in the life of the family meant that there was to be, in fact, a gap of seven years between the first children of the family and the last three. Although Robert, or Stephe as he was known, would go out with his elder brothers on occasions, in effect there were inevitably two family groups.

This Robert Stephenson Smyth, who was to become the great Baden-Powell, was born on 22 February 1857. Less than two years later came the birth of Agnes Smyth on 16 December 1858. It seems that the two middle children were sent away to their maternal grandparents for the event as, on the day of the birth, the ten-year-old George wrote to Frank (Francis), who was seven,

> We all hope that you are enjoying yourselfs at St. John's Lodge. Mama has the little baby and it is a girl. Stevenson has a little cold. We all hope you and Augustus have had a pleasant journy. I only write this note to tell you that the baby is born. Please give my best love to Grandpapa and Grandmama and Aunt Carry.

Obviously the family was to be all together for Christmas as, a few days later, George wrote again to Frank,

We all hope you are quite well and have not had such bad weather as we have had. We are going to have a Christmas tree. Warrington and I are waiting till the rain is over to go and tell Mr. and Mrs. Niven about the new baby and we are also going to tell the Miss Rivazs about the new baby, who live at Westminster.

There was to be one more addition to the family: Baden Fletcher Smyth was born in May 1860. By this time Baden Henry was nineteen years old and had been away from the family home since his father's marriage to Henrietta. It could be that his step-mother wanted a child of her own named after the husband she adored and that, as Baden Henry would be going to India, there would be little chance of the duplication being noticed. She was to have more need of Baden Henry's legal expertise than she realised.

Baden was born at 6 Stanhope Street, on the eastern side of Regents Park. This had become the family's home a few years before when Baden's radical thinking had made Oxford too hot for him to continue living there with his family, although he retained his Professorship. On the occasion of this birth the two eldest boys, Warington and George, seem to have stayed at home, presumably so that they could continue to attend St Paul's School, while all the rest of the family was packed off to their ever helpful grandparents at St John's Lodge in Aylesbury. It was here that the ten-year-old Augustus assumed the responsibilities of the eldest. Augustus was an affectionate and imaginative child who shared with his next brother, George, a great love of natural history. As the eldest at St John's Lodge, he assumed the responsibility of writing to his parents on behalf of all the younger ones. On 16 May he wrote to his mother,

This note is written to tell you how well we all are. And to know how you, dearest papa, George and Warrington are? Please are we to have [?] money while we are here? Stephenson and Agnes have not been out for it rains so all day. We are so very sorry to hear that dear Papa had taken a chill on Wednesday. I am so happy to here [sic] that Warrington and George have won in the cricket match. Please tell George that I have 2 birds eggs that I think he has not. It is now Post time and 8 o'clock this morning when I write this note. I am your aft son Augustus Smyth Powell P.S. Little Agnes is just going to have an egg for her breakfast.

Later on the same day he wrote to his father,

I am happy to tell you that we all arrived quite safe, and Agnes seems to be very happy tho they cannot go out for it rains so very hard. Please dear Papa excuse the blots for Agnes has made them. Please do [?] ma to. Write and tell me how you and mama are? We shall long so to know. I am making my gardens very nice, dear Papa. I must leave for now it is Post time.

A couple of days later he wrote again to his mother. After asking for news, and before telling of his latest exploration into the world of birds, he slips in the information,

. . . Please tell dearest Papa that Agnes and Stephenson are quite well and happy they have such a nice colour in their faces . . .

There is one more letter written by Augustus at this time. On 20 May, when there was still no sign of the baby's arrival, he wrote again to his father, using a pen that was obviously desperately in need of a new nib, and assured his father that Agnes and Stephenson were well. Baden was born two days later.

On 29 May Augustus wrote to his mother a letter that included a drawing he had done of St John's Lodge. Agnes, at seventeen months old, was at that glorious age when every day shows some new development, and it must have been heartbreaking for such loving parents to miss out on it. However, Augustus assured them that, 'Agnes knows where is her head, her ears, her eyes, her nose, her tongue.' The grandparents were obviously having a wonderful time with the children.

The chill after which Augustus enquired did not get better. Baden had been suffering since April from breathlessness and chest pains. Yet such was his love for his children that he continued to write to them and, on at least one occasion, to send them some very amusing silhouette animals cut out of scrap paper. On 31 May Augustus wrote,

. . . Please ask Warry and George to write the news about dearest Papa I am afraid he is very ill. I think it will Please him to think that Stephenson and Agnes are quite well and happy . . .

On 9 June the children, clutching the silhouettes of animals which he had cut out for them, were taken to see their father. On 11 June, three weeks after the birth of little Baden, he died aged sixty-four. The thirty-five-year-old Henrietta was a widow with seven children and little income.

The cut-out animals exist to this day, stored in an envelope in the family archives. Each of them is cut out in double paper, so that they can stand up. The envelope is made out of mourning writing paper, and on it Henrietta Grace has written,

These animals are some of those which my dearest cut out and sent only a few days before his death, to his children, then at St John's Lodge Augustus – Frankie – Stephenson – Agnes. They happened to bring these home to Stanhope Street, when they came up to see their dear Father, two days before his death.

A ONE-PARENT FAMILY

The first issue which Henrietta had to address was that of finance. She and her husband both came from reasonably comfortable backgrounds and she was determined that her children should have nothing less. That would require money and contrivance.

Financial needs applied only to Henrietta and her children, since Baden's family from his marriage to Charlotte had inherited a comfortable sum from their mother. Accordingly, as far back as 1851 there had been correspondence between Professor Powell and his solicitor securing as much as possible to Henrietta.

When Baden's affairs were settled it seemed that the family would have an investment income of between £700 and £800 a year. This may not seem a lot but, in 1860, it was not abject poverty. From her husband, Henrietta inherited £2,000 in 3 per cent Great Western

Debentures and family land in Kent which, until sold in 1863, would bring in a further £6,300. In addition, Baden's two single sisters who lived in Speldhurst, near Tunbridge Wells, gave £2,000. Then there was the income from Henrietta's own marriage settlement of £5,000. The lease on the house in Stanhope Street was put into a trust for the children, thereby starting what was to be a lifetime of using property to generate income. Other small amounts would be added to the income as family members died and left legacies to Henrietta.

It was seen in a letter which Augustus wrote home that the children were used to receiving some sort of pocket money. Henrietta now introduced a form of communal family finance which must have been as radical then as it would seem now, and which would moderate the family's fortunes for the rest of Henrietta's life. On a table in the hall was placed a small metal box of money and, from it, the children would take such money as they required, leaving a receipt. For instance, Stephe's commonest receipt used to read, 'Orange £0/0/1'.

Financial help continued to be given by members of the family and, in particular, Baden's sisters in Speldhurst. On one occasion Aunt Em wrote to Agnes, who was not quite five,

> My dear little [no big] Azzie, I hear from Mama that Azzie wants a new frock so you ought to have asked Mama to put it down on her list; for she certainly ought to have one for the winter if she wants it, as well as her Mama . . .

She goes on to ask that one of her existing dresses should be posted to Speldhurst so that her aunt can get one in the exact size. The sisters' generosity to the family had certainly not ended with the death of their brother.

In order that Henrietta and Agnes could live in the style to which Henrietta was sure they should be accustomed, and that all the boys should be launched on their careers, their communality would continue. Each of the children had a £2,000 legacy from their father, in trust until their majority. However, as each of them reached twenty-one, their mother made clear the expectation that it would be handed over for the benefit of whoever most needed it at that time. Of course they all complied.

But the support given by the boys was to continue beyond that. Once they embarked upon their careers, 50 per cent of their income was handed over into the family coffer. This meant that none of them were able to marry until middle age, something that was resented especially by Warington's wife, Hilda, who, by the time they married after a courtship exceeding twenty years, was no longer able to have children.

The next thing to be settled was housing. No.6 Stanhope Street was only leasehold and it was expensive. Early in March 1862 the family moved to No.1 Hyde Park Gate in Kensington, also leasehold, where they would stay for some years. Writing to her mother after she had secured the house, Henrietta wrote that No.1 Hyde Park Gate

> is small and retiring – fit for a widow with small means and for one servant to clean; yet, with bedrooms enough for my many boys. There are [kitchens below]
> 2 sitting rooms on entering
> 3 bedrooms over them
> 4 bedrooms at the top
> The air must be almost as fresh as country – so many gardens are round about, besides the Park . . . I do indeed hope and trust that we may have been led to decide aright, though it is by no means <u>exactly</u> what I wanted. We have engaged it from Michaelmas next, so as to give time for this house to let, if possible before I need to pay rent for the other

As the family moved six months ahead of Michaelmas it can be assumed that the house in Stanhope Street was let very speedily, probably to the relief of all concerned.

Then there was the matter of the children's education. All of them had had their early education at home from their parents. Until his death their father would take them for walks in the park and read to them so as to arouse their interest in books. Fraulein Groffel, a German governess, was with them for many years and there had been a French governess. Overall their education had been intelligent and broad, and it probably helped to make them the strong people they each became. By the time of their father's death the older boys were at St Paul's

School. However, the matter of fees had to be considered and, after the death of two of their fellow pupils, they were moved to Marlborough School which offered reduced fees for sons of the clergy.

The younger children continued to be educated at home. They were taught reading, writing and singing by their mother and Fraulein Groffel, and their mother also taught them dancing and exercise. During the holidays a tutor would come to stay who taught Mathematics, Greek and Latin. Each evening they would sit with Henrietta while they did their drawing; they would then go into the Library and work with the Governess while Henrietta ate her supper. In due course, and after beating on a number of doors, Henrietta managed to gain for Stephe and Baden free Gownboy places at Charterhouse School.

With all her brothers at school Agnes must have felt very lonely. It was a time when serious schools for girls were burgeoning. Her mother was very keen on the idea; she was particularly keen on High Schools and became a Committee member of the Girls' Public Day School Trust. However, any available money was being used for the education of the boys, as they were the ones who would need to have careers, so Agnes continued to be educated at home. It must have been a grave disappointment to both mother and daughter. Nevertheless, that education was by no means deficient and, as we shall see, Agnes grew up to be an incredibly talented woman. By the age of six-and-a-half she was able to write a three-page letter to her mother using the classic German script.

AUGUSTUS

Augustus, the third of the Powell boys, was just eleven when his father died. His letters show an attractive boy who had great affection for his family. Like all intelligent little boys of that age he had enthusiasms, especially for natural history and making things.

By the time we meet him again he is making a prolonged stay with his father's sisters in Speldhurst, Kent, and he is very sick. In fact he was suffering from tuberculosis and being with his aunts would enable him to be away from London to take full advantage of the fresh country air which was the newest treatment for the disease. His mother must have delivered him to Speldhurst at the beginning of March 1862 for, on the 3rd of that month, he wrote her a long letter:

> After you had gone on Friday I went and laid down on my bed for an hour and a half. On Saturday I made Cousin Charlie 16 trays for the Cabinet which we are to fill with birds' eggs, if we can, and on Monday I am to make two more and then I shall have filled one drawer. Aunt Emily measure's out my quinine every day, I take it twice in the day and once at night. Aunt Emily has kindly made me a new neck tie. I have not been out yet, but hope to go to day as the weather is a little finer. How are the dear boys, are they quite well? I hope so, and that you, Warrington, Stephenson, Agnes and Baden are all quite well also. Please donot forget to put my little white closet with two daw's in my room and do not let Frank open the birds eggs which we got at St. John's Lodge till I come home.

Later that day he writes,

> Yesterday Mr. Saint and Mr. Pott. Aunt Emily told Cousin Charlie and me to go into the diningroom and seat ourselves before they came in, when Mr. Saint came in he said O hear is the invalid and then came round the table and said How do you do Gustus, I hope you are stronger now. I sat next to Mr. Saint and Mr. Pott sat opposite me, then after dinner I laid on Aunt Emily's couch, I went out into the garden, then I came in at half past 3 oclock went to sleep and at 6 oclock I went down to tea in the diningroom, then after tea I went into Aunt Susan and Eleanor Drawing room and fell fast asleep till bed time . . .

From this we learn how ineffective the treatment of TB was in those days. It is also interesting to note that Augustus was mixing with his cousin (the son of his father's younger brother, Charles, and of a similar age to Augustus) and visitors, which seems to indicate little knowledge of the degree of infection carried by TB. Being packed off to the country, as we have noted, was the recognised treatment at that time, but the separation must have been very difficult for his mother, as well as his siblings, although Henrietta must have felt unable to cope with an invalid in the midst of her young family.

Correspondence was obviously frequent and hampers went back and forth, presumably on the train. Augustus sent a gift to his mother for her wedding anniversary, in reply to which he received a very affectionate letter:

> My darling Son Augustus   Thank you very much for your loving remembrance of my dear wedding day; it was a sad day for me to think how many happy anniversaries I have had of this day and that I can never have such happiness again on this earth . . .

Henrietta goes on to thank him for his loving letters and 'the most beautiful mat', adding, 'I think Aunt Emily or Aunt Eleanor must have worked three fourths of it, and you the other fourth. I should like to put it under glass, it looks so pretty.'

Following their move to No. 1 Hyde Park Gate, Henrietta goes on to tell Augustus how the boys get to school as easily from the new address, although it takes a little longer. They were at St Paul's School which, in those days, was close to St Paul's Cathedral. The three youngest children had been at St John's Lodge for the move, or while arrangements had been made for Augustus, or both, for his mother writes that they are to return home on the 22 March. Augustus could barely wait to know that they were home for, on the 23 March, he wrote to his mother,

> Please kiss each of the little ones when they come home on Monday if I write to Stephenson do let him open it and read it to himself. Cousin Charlie will send Agnes a little book in the next hamper. Yesterday Mr. Duncan came and told Aunt Emily that I was to take 5gms Rhubarb, 5gms Soda, and 3gms ginger this morning so I took it and it made me so sleepy that I have been in bed all day until now, half past four.

One also learns that Aunt Eleanor has asked him for a drawing and that Frank has been dilatory in finding a box that Augustus wanted.

The next incident of note happened at the beginning of April. Henrietta wrote, apologising for not having written for some time and explaining that she had had a sore throat which made her feel too unwell to write (this would continue to happen throughout her life). The three little ones are not yet home and no date has been fixed for their return.

By this time Warington, who had always been keen on boats, had decided that he wished to go to sea. He was on the training ship *Conway* in Liverpool, and there exciting things were happening. Henrietta wrote to Augustus,

> Now I have some excellent news from the *Conway* to tell you, and I hope that you will then tell it to your dear Aunts and Uncle Charles, for if Warry had not been so sturdy, it would have been a sad blow to me just when I felt weak, had he been sent home, expelled! This has been the sorrow which has come upon four poor mothers this week.
>
> On Tuesday last, a boy on the *Conway* had behaved so ill that Capt. Roger had him flogged. The other boys thought the flogging was not deserved so, in order to show their disapproval, numbers of the boys united to get up what they called a 'row', but what I call a mutiny. They put out all the lights, smashed the lamps, and continued noise and confusion all through Wednesday morning. 'Suddenly' says Warry 'there was a stillness all through the ship, and a report ran round that the Committee came on board. Warry does not say how many – but I dare say that Sam Rathbone and the Mayor of Liverpool headed it. Everyone was full of awe, and silence reigned every where. They had come like a court martial, to settle whether even the Captain himself had done right, and to sift every particular of every person on board.
>
> Their first demand was that the Captain should write down the names of the three most trustworthy lads out of the hundred. So he wrote down
>
> > Warington Powell
> >
> > Lister
> >
> > Lunn
>
> Each of these three boys had then to be examined singly and alone before the Committee.
>
> Finally – in the afternoon all hands were piped on deck. There were all the Committee, the Captain – the officers, the school masters, the sailors of the ship and all the *Conway* boys assembled together

to hear the judgement. This was that the 4 boys were to be at once publicly expelled. Warry says of course he took care to keep out of this because the Committee had said last half that they expected entire obedience from the boys to the Captain.

Henrietta had once again used the influence of one of the friends who she cultivated so assiduously to gain for Warington his place on the *Conway*, so obviously he would do his best to keep out of trouble. Nevertheless, the approach of such a loving mother to the whole event gives a clear indication of what was acceptable discipline at that time. However, the Committee minutes covering the affair must have made interesting reading.

By 10 April, the children were at last home from their grandparents and Henrietta was able to forward a drawing which Stephenson had done for Augustus and to give news of little Baden. Agnes was by then three and her mother wrote,

Agnes looks as well as possible – still very tiny and ladylike – so sweet tempered, she does whatever I tell her, that instant, with such a pleasant quiet look. She sings to her doll about Little Bo Peep. The greatest change that I observe in her is her speaking so much more distinctly than she did . . .

At the beginning of August, Henrietta had obviously had a rainy holiday in Scotland and two of the babies were once again staying with their grandparents at St John's Lodge. Augustus wrote,

Tell George that two Sunday's ago I caught a Golden crested wren. I kept it alive for a day but it would die, so it did, it was too young to stuff. Do not forget to ask Warington for my winch and my swivel like this [both sketched] Please bring them home with you when you come, the winch I want is the small one with silk running line on it the which Don wants. Now I want to get the soft side of you for I want you to spare me two little split rings for fastening on the tables of keys like this [sketched] Could you send them in your next letter, they are this size O do dear do Please . . .

Dear Augustus, gallant to the end. He was to live for another eight months, dying on 3 April 1863. What a terrible time it must have been for all the family, especially for his mother. She wrote in one of her letters to him of having gone into his room (the room he had never used) to watch the sun rise; was this an attempt to be near her son after a sleepless night?

Even then the family was not free of the scourge of tuberculosis. The sixteen-year-old George was infected, although perhaps not so seriously. A different type of air was to be tried and so he was sent on a cruise and this treatment worked: he recovered. The family's worst troubles were over and they could begin to move forward.

GROWING UP
The Right House

Even today it is not unusual for a woman who is newly widowed to have no experience of financial management. In the mid-nineteenth century, when a woman and her possessions were regarded as part of her husband's chattels, this was even more the case. The young Henrietta Powell was fortunate in having helpful relatives in both her own and her husband's family; nevertheless, she needed to assume the financial reins. She was a woman who knew where her family should go and the achievement of her goals rested with her.

The first move, in March 1862, to No. 1 Hyde Park Gate, one of the roads running south from Kensington Gardens, was to quite a good address; a century later it was to be the street where Winston Churchill lived for his last years. The house was large enough for each member of the family to have their own room and to accommodate one maid. The number of reception rooms was the minimum which was acceptable but, as we have said, in a letter to her mother, written before the move, she described it in 'adequate' terms.

As any householder knows, the outgoings on one's home make constant demands and they are not balanced by any compensatory income. Henrietta was holding together her family on a tight budget and needed to find a way for the house to pay for itself. The means she discovered rested on her knowing the right people and, fortunately, she did. During the Season it was normal for fashionable families to move into furnished accommodation in and near Mayfair and, very often, the houses into which they moved had been vacated by the families who normally lived there. This was obviously the solution.

Thus began the years of wandering, when the family would spend their summers staying with friends or relatives, or in boarding houses. It gave them an opportunity to explore the country and, in doing so, to meet many interesting people. With the older boys safely at boarding school there was no fear of disruption in the children's education for, by the time they broke up for their summer holidays, the Season would be over. Henrietta could continue the younger children's education and, when he became ready for something more, Stephe could be accommodated in some local school where they were staying. For instance, in 1867 the family stayed at Winnington Hall, an unconventional girls' boarding school in Cheshire where the Headmistress was Miss Margaret Bell. The ten-year-old Stephe attended a nearby school which was run by a clergyman. It was during this time that the family was introduced to John Ruskin who was, at that time, the visiting art teacher at Winnington Hall. He was much attracted to the little Agnes; he wrote to her for some time and even invited her to visit him at Denmark Hill.

The stay at Winnington Hall would have been enjoyed particularly by Henrietta with her fascination for girls' education and her membership of the Council of the Girls' Public Day School Trust. It must have been a great disappointment to her that she was unable, presumably for financial reasons, to send Agnes to school. Nevertheless, the theories which underlaid girls' education at the time obviously underlaid the classical, but broad, education which Agnes received.

By 1877, with all the boys off her hands and with more income, Henrietta was able to contemplate another move for herself and her daughter. Sometime between 1877 and 1879 the move was made to No.8 St George's Place, at Hyde Park Corner. Here, again, it was possible for each member of the family to have their own room, offering sufficient space for them to enjoy their hobbies. Agnes had room for her embroidery frames, her pressed flowers and her beehives. There would also be a garden where Agnes was able to spend hours tending her beloved herb garden. The house was also in a more fashionable area of London, offering even more facility for letting, should the need arise.

However, by that time the older members of the family were beginning to make careers in London and it would probably have been even more inconvenient to vacate the house each summer than when they were at school. At that address all London came to call. Henrietta and Agnes knew most of the intelligentsia and were popular.

The single members of the family continued to live in St George's Place until the family's final move. In 1902 the Piccadilly Line of the London Underground, or the 'Tuppenny Tube' as it was known, was being built and the family home in St George's Place was too close for comfort to the new Hyde Park Corner Station. The hunt for a suitable new house had already started in 1899. Eventually the decision was taken to move back to the area south of Kensington Gardens. The address chosen was No.32 Princes Gate, a small turning off Exhibition Road, just near to the new Albert Hall. It was to here that the family moved in the middle of November 1902. Henrietta, by then in her seventies, had been packed off, possibly to Brighton, when the initial work was done, and Agnes masterminded the rest, so we have some knowledge of the way in which it was spread over a couple of days. Agnes put Henrietta and some of her friends on the train and wrote to her later,

> I very nearly turned round, to get in and come too. I thought I had better, and then I didn't. Then went to my Committee, met . . . and lots of others. On coming out into the dark and rain I was quite puzzled where to go home to, and thought to go back to you, and then I thought wherever it is, you were not there, it was terrible.

Two days later, on 14 November, Agnes sent her mother an update. She was obviously exhausted. She wrote,

> All the men have been and all the things done, that were to be. The Auxiliary have cleared the Hall!! the bottles are gone! drawing room pictures hung!! . . . dining room curtains and swords up.

She had dealt with the post, including forwarding letters to Warington, and had been let down at the last moment by people who had not said definitely whether they would call. Baden, however, went to the Mercers dinner and brought back sweets in a silver dish. I was glad of a quiet evening as I have really had no time to breathe.

By the time Agnes wrote her second letter, her mother had moved to another hotel. What was wrong with the Grand? On 26 November Henrietta had been expected home but Agnes was writing to ask if she should come and collect her.

At the time of the December quarter day in 1911 the owner of the lease, Ed Heywood, wrote a memorandum giving the recent history of the letting of the house and presenting the lease to the four Baden-Powells still living at home: Warington, Stephenson, Agnes and Baden. This remained in their gift until their death. This generous act had the additional advantage of giving the family some income as stables were attached. The annual rent for one of the stables was £20 and, if all were let, the £100 income would pay the Ground Rent on the house. However, as all were riders, the stables were presumably used by the family.

FINANCE

It is one thing to live on a tight budget; it is another to announce the fact to the whole world, especially when one is living on the edge of the smart set. Henrietta had a problem and she resolved it with her usual resourcefulness.

As we know, the family practised a common purse. This was to continue into adulthood. There was no other way in which it would be possible for a home to be maintained for Henrietta and Agnes, and for any other sons who might be in England.

All but one of the sons lived away from home for at least some of their time. Warington and George both went into the Navy before coming back to London to enter the Law. Stephe and Baden both entered the Army and remained overseas for most of the time until early in the twentieth century. Frank was the only member of this artistically talented family to go into art professionally. But the women still needed an income and girls of Agnes' upbringing did not go out to work, unless it was to the drudgery of being a governess, and Agnes was wanted at home far too much for that, for she had been playing a major part in the housekeeping since she was fifteen.

The scheme which was devised for the maintenance of the home and the women of the family was one which was to have repercussions on all the boys. In the first place, as each of the children reached twenty-one and inherited the £2,000 left to them by their father, this money was taken into the common purse and used for whichever family member had most need of it. Secondly, as has already been stated, each son was required to pay into the family exchequer half of his income.

The result of this on the members of the family can be readily imagined. Stephe, for instance, as an army officer, was never able to keep up with his colleagues in his expenditure. None of the boys were able to marry until they were well established in their careers. In the case of Warington, the eldest, it meant that when eventually he was able to marry his sweetheart of more than twenty years, it was too late for them to have children. One can understand the lasting bitterness which his wife felt about this. But the scheme worked and Henrietta and Agnes had a good home in which every member of the family had their own space.

WHAT'S IN A NAME?

Anybody with the name of Powell will tell you that they are part of a very long list in the telephone book. Henrietta had admired and adored her husband and she was determined that his memory would be perpetuated in her children. The way in which she resolved this was to incorporate his Christian name of Baden into the family surname. Thus, in 1869, the family name became Baden-Powell by means of a public notice.

Henrietta was fiercely protective about this new name, so much so that members of the wider family came to refer to her as 'Old Mother Hyphen'. The new surname was to be used only by those of Baden's children who had been born to her. Thus Baden's children of his second marriage were pushed even further out of the family circle. Dissent continues to this day between those who consider their use of the name to be legitimate and those who are not considered to have the right to use it. Eventually Stephe's wife, Olave, passed on the letters patent for the hyphen (together with her magnifying glass) to George's son, Donald.

A WEALTH OF KNOWLEDGE

There are some very strange ideas about the inadequacies of Victorian education. Yet this was an age of exploration. Agnes was born at the other end of the decade in which the Great Exhibition had been held in Hyde Park. Almost certainly her parents would have attended that. Moreover her father was an Oxford Professor and her mother was very interested in science and girls' education. There could be no way in which Agnes' home education would be inferior in any way to that of her brothers. Indeed, it could be argued that it may well have been superior. Under the guidance of her mother and her German governess, Agnes' alert mind absorbed a wealth of knowledge.

Like all Victorian girls, Agnes learned music. The instrument on which she excelled was her violin. However, she also became proficient on the piano and the organ and is reputed to have mastered another four instruments. Most evenings, after dinner, the family would repair to the music room where they would play their own and each other's instruments, and sing part songs. On other occasions there was acting, but this the shy Agnes refused to do.

It would seem that she had a natural aptitude for languages – the eleven which she learned included Latin, Greek, Hebrew and Persian, as well as modern languages. About the time of her twentieth birthday, she made a chart of the hours spent each day over a period of four months in the study of Greek. On occasions the number of hours in one day would be as many as five.

One of Agnes' great passions was natural history. She kept bees in the sitting room, in a hive which she had made to her own design, of mahogany with a glass front. The entrance to the hive was fitted through the window but inevitably some of the bees must have got into the room on occasions. In the hall Agnes kept her colony of birds, including up to twenty-one canaries which lived in a bay window on the stairs. For many years she had a tame sparrow which went around the house on her shoulder. Somewhere in the house she kept her unique flock of butterflies. She had a love of botany, pressing flowers and became extremely knowledgeable in the subject.

Her ability at all forms of handicraft was outstanding. She won awards for her repoussé work. This is a form of metalwork in which the design is beaten out. A repoussé work mirror which she had made, and which was probably a competition piece, came to auction in a television antiques show in 2006 and sold for £260. The circular wooden plaque which backed the mirror would also have been made by Agnes, for she had certificates in woodwork too. She was also proficient in lace making, and collected old lace; indeed, she delighted in all forms of needlework. And, as well as all of this, she had, like the rest of the family, inherited her father's ability in art. The volumes of her paintings which remain are of an amazingly high standard.

It can hardly be expected that the one sister in a family of boys would remain uninterested in sport. Agnes' love of exercise remained with her to the end of her life and, in Guiding, found expression in the camping which she loved. And so, with her brothers, Agnes learned to swim, to skate, to cycle and, eventually, to drive and to fly, as well as the more normal social sports of riding, fishing and shooting.

A LADY OF MANY TALENTS

Very little is known of Agnes until she was in her forties. The family home, near Hyde Park Corner, was on the edge of the fashionable part of London. While the boys made their way in their careers, Henrietta launched Agnes into Society. They went everywhere and met everyone. Henrietta even managed the expense of Agnes' presentation at Court. But in all things there was the constant issue of financial ways and means, and of course Agnes had no dowry or independence of her own. She needed to use her own resources to fill her life and in that she succeeded admirably.

A lady who has grown up as the only girl in the midst of a family of boys may be either a tomboy or a complete girl. Agnes managed to achieve both. On the one hand she was incredibly talented in all forms of art and craft; at the same time she was a keen and competent sportswoman. It is obvious that Agnes' many gifts were recognised by those who met her. When she was in her thirties a Mr Macgregor, a man who was deeply committed to encouraging people to help in the development of the colonies, would write to her brother,

> Like anyone else, I am profoundly impressed with the extraordinary versatile talents of Miss Baden-Powell. What a pity it is that her abilities are masked here instead of being turned to account in a new country.

Music was a compelling force within the family, as it is still for members of the Baden-Powell family. It is not surprising, therefore, to learn that there was a music room in the house and that music-making was the family's preferred way of spending an evening together. Baden and Henrietta had both been keen musicians and it would have been odd if at least some of their children had not imbibed their interest in the subject. This was, of course, before the days of Associated Board exams; nevertheless, Agnes is reported to have been proficient in no less than seven instruments. Learning to play the piano and to sing was an essential element of the education of any little girl of Agnes' background and it is known that her mother was her music teacher. In addition we are told that Agnes was an excellent violinist and also proficient on the organ. For the other instruments she probably learned to play those used by other members of the family. She would certainly never hold back if there was a challenge in the offing.

Like many musical people, Agnes was also a proficient linguist, as we know. In later years she was to join the Dante Society which was dedicated to English and Italian conversation. This may also have been an offshoot of her friendship with Marconi of whom she was a great admirer. There is extant a letter of congratulations which she wrote to him after he had 'bridged the Channel' and it is quite obvious that they were already well acquainted. He was a frequent visitor to the house. In March 1899 Agnes wrote to her mother, who was visiting a sick friend,

Not many visitors, but Saturday suddenly was announced Mr. Marconi, so he came to spend the day, he said he had three hours to spare so thought he would call! He is so nice and so modest, I felt quite abashed to have such celebrity all to myself. We tried every subject and we had tea, and then he played Mascagni on the organ, at least strummed! He wants to send me tickets for his lecture, he wants to fix a day for you to come to tea with him at the T. Station near Poole, and see the instruments, he told me a lot of interest about his fortnight with the Prince of Wales on the yacht – sending all their little chat by vibrations to Osborne, only the Prince begged 'for goodness sake don't telegraph it Q. just the Queen'. They all have pet names for each other and the royalties all call Marconi, Maccaroni.

It is rumoured that Marconi once proposed to Agnes. What is certain is that she attended his wedding, after which she wrote to her mother,

Signor Marconi's wedding was also a wonderful scene. The whole of George Street a mass of crowd, seas of faces, the whole road full. As I was slowly driving up to the door in line I saw Marconi himself come past in a hansom, with a quietly amused smile of astonishment on his face. No one knew him and he went by a back street to the vestry. All the family went by the back door, rather a good dodge. When I got there, 35 minutes before the time, every pew was full, except the outer wall row. But didn't the crowd cheer and cheer him as he came out!! ... The guests all got away quickly by the clergy door, a splendid plan.

Natural history was important to Agnes and this is hardly surprising in one who loved being out-of-doors. The family had a collection of butterflies but there were also live butterflies flying around the house. Anyone going into the hall would be confronted by un-caged birds flying around. Indeed, for many years Agnes had a tame sparrow which used to follow her around, perch on her shoulder and feed from her hand. It would seem that other members of the family were given birds for, on one occasion, Agnes wrote,

Please ask Maud [George's daughter and, therefore, her niece] to seriously think what name her bird had better have as it is getting very difficult for him to live without a name. He is singing beautifully, and can quack like a duck, too. Would 'Felix' do?

On another occasion, while staying with her sister-in-law, Frances, in Cheltenham, Agnes wrote to her mother expressing her concern for the welfare of her birds,

> I do hope the little birds get seed and water, especially in the big breeding cage, and where they can get at it. Also does Ecc. water the palm, and the plants in Boudoir?

This was not the only livestock for, in the sitting room, Agnes kept a hive of bees. These appear to have been in various hives over the years. At one time they were in a series of mahogany beehives which she had made to her own design. At another time their hive was made of glass, which must have provided constant interest for those in the room. Whatever the type of hive, the inside was always connected to the world outside by a metal tube which was fitted through the window. However, nervous visitors must have been pacified by the opportunity to look at Agnes' collection of pressed flowers. They would also have welcomed an opportunity to taste some of Agnes' prizewinning honey. On one occasion, after returning home from a visit, she wrote to her mother,

> . . . the Little Bees was humming gaily, and seem very content, bringing in quantities of pollen in lumps on their legs.

Like at least two of her brothers, Agnes had inherited their father's artistic ability. Her watercolours in later years were to be much appreciated by many of her friends. Beehives were not the only things she created from wood and she was awarded certificates for her woodwork. In metal, too, she was adept. She was certificated in the art of steel engraving and was a medallist in repoussé, a kind of beaten metal work. In 2006 a circular mirror which Agnes had made, of a repoussé work surround on a polished wooden base, was sold in a television antiques auction for £260. This was probably a competition piece as there was a label on the back giving her name.

What might be thought of as 'softer' pastimes were also of interest to Agnes. She both made and collected lace, she enjoyed all forms of needlework and she did calligraphy. On one occasion, while staying in Wokingham, she wrote to her mother that her host, Mr Noble, was teaching her to make screws in his workshop.

But, as has been mentioned, this only girl in a family of brothers was also an enthusiast for most forms of sport, including some which would be considered unusual, even today. In a letter from Suffolk, written in 1900, she talks of sailing, cycling, tennis and golf, and she was a visitor to Cowes. This is one of the occasions when her letter to her mother shows that being able to afford the right clothes for all her activities was a consideration.

In 1898 Agnes has been fishing and, on another occasion, she writes of house parties where there has been hunting and shooting. Cycling was one of her passions: she was a keen player of bicycle polo and one of the best known pictures of her shows Agnes on her bike and surrounded by a big hoop, looking as though she is about to take part in a bicycle obstacle race. In fact, she used to cycle through the hoop. Many years later, in the Girl Guide pages in *Home Notes*, a contemporary was to print the following article, illustrated by the famous picture:

There is no longer the great craze for bicycling which used to prevail. Among the greatest enthusiasts for performing on the wheel was Miss Baden-Powell, at a time when bicycle gymkhanas and races were all the rage. Many prizes in those contests fell to her share, and the delights of racing while kneeling on the saddle, or riding on the handle-bars, or standing on one peddle only, were among the lighter efforts of these Amazons of the wheel. In lemon cutting and tilting at the ring Miss Baden-Powell carried off many a prize, as also in that far more difficult feat of riding through the hoop. Taking a child's hoop in the right hand, she was expected to ride through it six times while guiding her machine within the chalked lines. Besides winning these competitions, Miss Baden-Powell has often been leader of the ladies' bicycle polo, being a bold and expert rider.

In September 1903 Maitre Felix Grave wrote to announce the reopening of his fencing salle. Many of these sports required the sort of finances the Baden-Powells' did not have and it is likely that, on frequent occasions, Agnes was reluctantly an onlooker or a supporter.

The camping which she had done with her brothers in childhood stayed with her; it was to remain one of her great loves throughout her life. While staying in Stevenage she wrote to her mother,

> It was so hot that the 2 Miss Baynes decided to camp out, so I went too and we slept in the garden, under the spreading branches of an ancient oak, which made quite a tent on the lawn. But the noises all round were so disturbing, cocks, thruses, dogs, thrushes etc. That we all came in at 4.30 a.m.

Science, too, came within Agnes' scope. Towards the end of his life her mother's brother, Professor Charles Piazzi Smyth, the former Astronomer Royal, wrote to her,

> My dear and clever Agnes Baden Powell, Your splendid example of Rontgen rays, is the most advanced in every way that I have yet seen. And I pity the owner of the hand exceedingly though he seems to keep up assurance and confidence grandly. I have not attempted anything in that way myself, and do not intend to try unless I can get the expenses paid, and have no hopes of that. But what are the Moving Photographs? I had not heard anything of them . . .

Agnes would have been in her late thirties at the time and, a short while before, had offered to go and stay for a while with her elderly uncle who had recently been widowed.

UP, UP AND AWAY

However, Agnes' most momentous activities took place in the air. Very early on in its history, Baden became interested in flying. In the Boer war he had experimented with some success in the use in warfare of man-lifting kites. He became well known as a balloonist and he was frequently accompanied by Agnes. Together they made the balloons, Agnes' particular task being to work on the envelopes, for which she had obtained the silk. Obviously her skill with the needle was coming in very useful.

With the arrival of the aeroplane, they added this to their flying activities. Agnes would travel round seeking engines which were light enough to be used, and she was adept at stripping down the engines.

In due course the Women's Aerial League was formed by Mrs Watt Smyth, under the Chairmanship of Lady O'Hagan. It was, not surprisingly, little time before Agnes was on both the Council and the Executive Committee.

The membership fee was one guinea, Associate membership was five shillings, and Honorary Associateship (entitled to literature only) was one shilling. The League had three objects: to encourage the invention of aerial craft, to disseminate knowledge, and to spread information showing the vital importance to the British Empire of aerial supremacy. Meetings were held over tea on Tuesday afternoons. The emphases appear to be aerial defence and the awarding of scholarships, although on at least one occasion the short talk on aviation was followed by a programme of music. Subjects covered included talks by ladies on their experiences of flying and a lecture on 'The Command of the Air'. On one occasion the League called a meeting 'to express public disapproval of the Government's persistent action of purchasing foreign air machines for the British Army'. On another occasion a banquet, which was attended by Baden, was held by the League. Only three ladies qualified as pilots during the first five years of organised aviation and, by 1914, there were no ladies flying at all.

The Women's Aerial League worked hard on the promotion of flying in general. Flying was encouraged among young people through the formation of the Boys' and Girls' Aerial League. In addition, a scheme was put to Baden-Powell for the formation of a Boy Scouts' Division of the Young Aerial League to offer to Scouts specially simplified aeronautical training. In due course this was to happen in the formation of the Air Scouts. The adults were encouraged, through the formation of a number of research scholarships at Imperial College, in the subjects of Physics, Chemistry or Engineering relating to aeronautics. The first scholarship was awarded to a Mr Bramwell who already had a distinguished career and who would carry out his research at the National Physical Laboratory. A Gold Medal was presented to a Mr

Grahame-White who, in his acceptance speech, stated that he valued it all the more as coming from the ladies who, his experience taught him, were possessed more of the type of courage required in aviation than was to be found in men!

A GROWING FAMILY

In April 1881 the Census shows four members of the family are resident in 8, St George's Place. All of them are unmarried. They are Warington, aged thirty-four, who gives his profession as Barrister at Law; George, aged thirty-three, who gives his profession as MA Political Author (Oxon.); Frank, aged thirty, who gives his profession as Artist. All of these give their place of birth as Oxford. Baden was also at home that night; aged twenty, he gave his place of birth as London Middlesex and his profession as 2nd Lieutenant Essex Militia. Also resident in the house were the forty-five-year-old cook, Elizabeth Watt, and the housemaid, Eliza Goodchild, who was twenty-nine. To find the ladies of the family on that night one has to go to the Great Malvern, Worcestershire, census where, at Knutsford Lodge, Abbey Road, are listed Harriet B. Powell, a widow of fifty-six, born in London, Middlesex, and who gives her profession as Boarder (Head) and Annuitant and her unmarried twenty-two-year-old daughter, Agnes, also born in London, Middlesex, and also a Boarder and Annuitant.

By this time Warington, at least, had met the woman he would eventually marry. However, marriage was out of the question for any of the men in the family. It was understood that all monies in the family were held in common. Each of the sons paid 50 per cent of his income into the family coffers in order that the family home and Henrietta and Agnes might be maintained in the manner to which they should be accustomed. Appearing to be better off than they were was part of Henrietta's strategy for helping her sons to get on in life. As for Agnes, it was obviously considered inappropriate that she should become a governess, the only type of work which would be open to her. Apart from anything else, her presence at home was of great value, especially as she gradually began to take on the running of the household.

Having served his time at sea in the Merchant Navy, Warington trained and then practised as a barrister. As the eldest son it was possibly considered preferable for him to be at home. However, he continued his boating activities for many years and was instrumental in the formation of the Sea Scouts. By the time he eventually married Cicely Farmer, known as Hilda, to whom he had been secretly engaged for over twenty years, he was sixty-six. The opportunity to have children had passed them by, something which Hilda never ceased to regret and for which she blamed Henrietta. They had had only nine years of married life when Warington died.

In most large families there is one member who chooses, to a greater or lesser extent, to distance themselves from the main body. The loner in this family seems to have been Francis, known as Frank. In a family where the artistic vein runs strongly he was the only one who chose to make his living by it, having initially trained for the Bar. He, too, was married at a later than usual age to Florence Nott, a wealthy New Zealander. Their one son, Bobby, was born in 1903. Not only did his marriage make him independent of the family but his artistic ability ensured that, during at least one period, Francis was the highest earner in the family.

In the summer of 1907 Agnes went with Frank and his family for a holiday in Sheringham. They travelled there by train and Agnes was quite shocked that Frank and Florence should choose to travel First Class when there was plenty of room in the Third Class carriage in which she travelled so comfortably. Despite the easier economic condition, the years of penury had taken their toll. Agnes took her dog, Pepin, with her, whose ticket on the train cost 2/6. In one of her letters to her mother she expressed surprise that a number of women were not wearing hats, while several others wore driving hats. The frequent letters home were concerned mainly with domestic matters and her mother's health.

Tim Jeal, in his biography of Robert Baden-Powell, mentions that Agnes stayed with Frank and Florence for a while after the death of their mother, but that this was not a success.

The life of Robert, known as Stephe, is well documented. His long army career, although he was impecunious because of his family responsibilities, was brilliant. After returning to England as the Hero of Mafeking he founded the Scouts and the rest, as they say, is history.

Agnes seems to have been closest to George and Baden. It will be recalled that, at the time of Baden's birth, it was George and Augustus who took such care of the little ones and sent regular reports from the home of their grandparents. George's career at Marlborough was much interrupted by the overseas travel which eventually cured his tuberculosis. Despite this, Benjamin Jowett saw enough potential in him to accept him at Balliol, his father's old college in Oxford. There he read History and set his sights on a political career.

George seems to have inherited much of his mother's adroitness in using his contacts in order to gain advancement. He worked assiduously, both as secretary or, as we would say today, researcher, to various people in public life and as a writer and journalist. In a bye-election in 1885 George at last achieved his ambition when he was elected the Unionist MP for one of the Kirkdale seats in Liverpool. By this time he had a great deal of successful work under his belt, including service on several commissions, especially in connection with the Colonial Service. It was very gratifying, therefore when, two years after his election to Parliament, George was knighted. George had always used his connexions, when necessary, to help his family and his sphere of influence was now widened. Now he was also in a position to entertain them, from time to time, at the House of Commons, which gave great pleasure.

In 1893 George married Frances Wilson who was welcomed cordially into the family. As MPs at that time were not paid until they reached the Front Bench, it was fortunate that Frances was wealthy. Their children, Maud and Donald, were born over the next four years and Aunt Azzie was to become very special to them. About the time of Donald's birth, George began to suffer from liver pains. A year later he died. History had repeated itself and once again a Baden-Powell had died leaving a young family. Donald wrote, many years later,

> He was the very best of company ... and was happiest in his own home ... for he was a devoted husband and father ... I never knew my father, yet I always felt his influence.

And in 1902 Henrietta was to write to Frances, who was very ill at the time,

The 'Garter' spoke reverently of dear George, remembered taking him to the Queen, and says that he had quite expected to give him the GCMG, and to see him Minister for the Colonies ...

Agnes received £500, a considerable sum by today's standards, in George's will.

Maud and Donald were two of the three grandchildren Henrietta was ever to know. Aunt Azzie, in particular, became very caring towards them, something that must have been welcomed by Frances who seems to have had very indifferent health. As Henrietta became increasingly housebound, Agnes must have felt very torn between the needs of, and love for, the two households. Two lovely items of correspondence with Donald are extant. The first is written on a postcard showing Robert Baden-Powell as the Hero of Mafeking and reads,

Miss Baden-Powell requests the honour of Mr. Donald Baden-Powell's company at dinner at 8 o'clock on Friday 5th October on the occasion of his 3rd Birthday. Should he unfortunately be previously engaged, she hopes he will transfer this invitation to the lady he loves best.

A few years later the six-year-old Donald laboriously wrote his aunt a letter, using all his coloured pencils, which she had apparently just sent him. He assured her that he did not smoke and told her that, as it was raining, he had had his hair cut. At the bottom of the letter he has drawn a picture with the caption, 'This is in a boat storm'. Artists start early.

The following year Frances had obviously written to Agnes to seek her advice about Maud who, at the age of ten, was growing 'wayward' and tending to be bossy with Donald. Henrietta replied to the letter, suggesting that Maud should go to boarding school and recommending Heathfield, a school of which many spoke well. In addition to its reputation was the financial consideration that the annual fees were only about £200, compared with the £300 charged by many schools. Henrietta pointed out that £200, was about the same annual sum as that required for a governess who would be paid £100 and have about £100 spent on her board and lodging. Frances, for whom financial considerations were less important, eventually chose Cheltenham Ladies' College which was certainly more convenient for home. In a later, undated letter, a much improved Maud is staying with her grandmother and aunt, charming family and friends alike with her pretty manners and her intelligence.

In 1909 Agnes spent a while staying with Frances in her home at Cheltenham. She writes of gardening with Donald and of Maud's wild flowers, and complains about a fellow guest who she describes as 'I, I, I'. It is also obvious from her letters that she is, by now, very much responsible for the housekeeping, for she sends instructions for the ordering of groceries and mentions how much meat is in the house. Henrietta, by then, would be in her late eighties. Agnes is eventually driven home when Frances, who has been confined to her room with a severe cold, talks of coming among her guests again, giving Agnes a fear of catching the germs.

In the summer of 1911 Agnes holidayed with the children in Felixstowe where Frances had apparently taken a house. There she was obviously the children's major companion. By then Maud was sixteen and Donald was rising fourteen, just at an age to enjoy all the things that Agnes had to share with them. They swam and drove and cycled, including Agnes teaching the children her famous trick of riding through a hoop. They sketched and made music and became very involved in the Beach Mission services which happened twice a day, even to making cakes for the special tea. It was obviously an idyllic summer.

The following summer there is a grateful letter of acknowledgement from Henrietta to Frances, after the arrival of her quarterly cheque for £50. The previous May, Agnes had written to Frances expressing disappointment that it was so long since the children had visited their grandmother. However, Frances may have been too ill to organise the visit for, in 1913, she too died. After this, for a while, Maud and Donald made their home with a relative in St Andrews where Maud attended the University. She read Hebrew (Aunt Azzie's influence?) and Chemistry before coming to London to study Medicine at the Royal Free Hospital. Medicine had been her original choice but Stephe, one of her Trustees, had forbidden it, so she had to wait until she was twenty-one. When Donald left Eton he went into the Army during the First World War; he was seriously wounded and invalided out, after which he, too, went up to Oxford. Maud and Donald never lost their deep affection for their beloved Aunt Azzie and remained in close contact with her.

However, there seems little doubt that the brother to whom Agnes was closest was Baden. As the baby of the family he shared their governess education with Agnes for three years longer than Stephe before following that brother to Charterhouse and then into the Army. He spent less of his military career overseas and served in several regiments. One of the most notable events of his career was being in the party which relieved Stephe at Mafeking in the middle of the night, having been given the privilege of going to wake his sleeping brother.

Upon his arrival back in England from South Africa, Baden decided to leave the Army and rely on his Major's pension to support him in the project of running a scientific journal called *Knowledge*. Unfortunately the journal rapidly lost both money and readers and Baden was saved from bankruptcy only by Frances' intervention. Throughout this time he was living at home where he proved a very popular uncle during the all too rare visits of his niece and nephews.

But the area in which Baden gained distinction, and an interest that he shared with Agnes, was in aviation. Mention has already been made of their ballooning exploits and of their early forays into flying. In the mid-1890s Baden had given a couple of lectures, which were printed, on the use of kites in warfare. He was an early member and benefactor of the Royal Aeronautical Society, being in turn its Honorary Secretary and then President. In 1897 he founded its technical journal, *The Aeronautical Journal*. Baden was also a member of the Aerial League of the British Empire, of which the Women's Aerial League was a branch, and was considered sufficiently important to be among the platform party at a public meeting held by them in 1910.

In later years Baden was to set up home at Riverhead, near Sevenoaks in Kent, where it was a great joy for his nieces and nephews, and also his great nieces and nephews, to go to stay with him. Here he had space for his frequent inventions, many of which were a source of great amusement. One invention cited by a niece was a gun that was powered by electricity. Unfortunately it was not a success as it tended to shoot round corners. Towards the end of his life Baden suffered from heart trouble. He died in 1937.

Some slight contact was kept with the members of Baden senior's family by his second marriage. Baden Henry inherited his father's love for mathematics, taking a First in the subject at Oxford where he, too, had attended his father's old college, Balliol. After giving such help to Henrietta with the administration of his father's estate, he made his career in the Indian Civil Service with great distinction, serving in Lahore from 1861 to 1889. He died in 1901 and in 1906 a brass tablet was unveiled to his memory in Lahore Cathedral.

FURTHER AFIELD

It would seem that, until Agnes was in her forties, Henrietta was disinclined to allow her too much independence. At the age of thirty-nine, while visiting in Wiltshire, Agnes became very friendly with an amateur archaeologist. She wrote to Warington requesting him to ask their mother if she might invite him to stay but the visit never happened. All this despite the fact that Agnes was taking increasing responsibility for the running of the house. Nevertheless, once past forty, Agnes started to travel more independently. Records of her visits to friends remain in the almost daily letters which she sent to her mother.

In 1887 Henrietta had just lost a long-running law suit. She had, to a certain extent, been living on expectations that she would receive a substantial inheritance from her much older sisters-in-law in Speldhurst. Possibly they considered that they had been sufficiently generous after Baden's death for, in the event, their estate had been left to relatives on the other side of the family. As a result of the law suit each member of the family was awarded £1,000, although presumably Henrietta would have had to pay the expenses. Severe retrenchment followed.

Stephe made mention, in a letter of the 1890s, to fun in 'the Malta days'. He was for a while ADC and Military Secretary to his uncle, General Smyth, who was the Governor at that time. In 1892-3 Henrietta and Agnes paid them a visit and, for a period, enjoyed the social whirl of the diplomatic life there. They also took the opportunity to go over to Algiers.

In 1895 Henrietta and Agnes, and possibly Warington, had been on holiday in Scotland. In *The Times* of 5 February in that year there was a paragraph which reads,

> Mrs. Baden-Powell, who met with a serious accident at Inverary, has now so far recovered as to have returned to her town residence, accompanied by Miss Baden-Powell and Mr. Warrington Baden-Powell.

By this time she would have been seventy and she seems to have travelled from home little after that.

In 1898 Agnes went to stay with a Mr and Mrs Knowles in Salisbury. Although her mother was not with her, Warington's long-suffering friend, Hilda Farmer, was. It was here that she struck up her friendship with Captain Hawley who was keen to take her to visit several local museums. Sadly this proved impossible when Henrietta forbade Agnes, who was in her fortieth year, to travel anywhere alone with the gentleman. Her initial reason for going seems to have been to see the 13th and 10th Hussars who were on exercises nearby. After going one evening to meet them the entire party set off in wagonettes the next morning after breakfast. Agnes wrote to Henrietta,

> . . . we saw bodies of troops moving in the far distance, then others galloped past us, 12 Lancers, lances glittering in the sun. We all got on a high barrow with the Hicks Beachs and neighbours. Then the masses of cavalry moved away south and began firing so we all scampered away to Stonehenge and saw a grand fight, and found Lord Wolsely, who nodded sweetly to me, and Sir Evelyn Wood and all the generals. Lord Dundonald told me he was camping in a wagon a mile from our house. Lady Lucy and Mrs Dickson (Brown) were photographing from Stonehenge. I spoke to Lord Wolsely who was most pleasant and said what an advantage the Kites would have been, then Lady Down and her daughter joined us and began talking about Stephe's diaries and how clever his sketches are. Lord Wolsely asked how Stephe liked India and said Lord Down is coming as umpire here. We got home to a late lunch, and then bicycled to a garden party, met the Hicks Beachs, rode home in torrents of rain, although I . . . had a mackintosh on, my

white dress was soaking wet and messed with lifting the machines and climbing over eight fences on the way home.

The next day they went again, with Captain Hawley following on foot, and cycled seven miles home in the middle of the afternoon. Agnes was invited by the Knowles to stay longer than originally intended and, as well as following the progress of the manoeuvres, Agnes took part in a tennis tournament, sketched, drove, played bicycle polo and fished. The weather was very mixed but she was finding the air extremely refreshing. This, of course, was the holiday when she went archaeology digging with Captain Hawley and she found it necessary to ask her mother to send her some wool stockings. She tells her mother all about what everyone is wearing for digging; she is wearing

the bluish 2/- blouse, and the old sage skirt, sometimes the pink silk skirt which is charming variety.

For general dress she says that the girls there,

wear hundreds of 2/- shirts and change several times a day. They wear low dresses in the evening, never the same one, all buttoned and chiffonier, so my old tab with pink frill daily, alternates with the lovely eau de nil once in a way. It is considered quite Parisian here.

In the evenings there was music. Agnes found little time for other activities after the long days out, although she must have found time for quite a bit of reading as Captain Hawley kept leaving archaeological books at her bedroom door. When they went shooting they found the stocks quite depleted because so many birds had been shot in the course of the army manoeuvres.

Eventually Henrietta decided to go and join Agnes for the final march past and received a horrified note pressing her not to come until the soldiers had finished, as the transport would be impossible until after they had gone. However, would her mother please bring some golf clubs and an itemised list of old clothes?

The following year Agnes, having reached the sensible age of forty, began to travel on her own. In the November she was holidaying in

Scotland, probably at Kelso, although she also stayed at Braco and Inchture. While at Kelso her mother wrote to her '. . . it will be too cold I fear for you to attempt to fish with Miss Radcliffe.'

Agnes was presumably staying in the same place when she wrote to her mother at the beginning of December on the subject of fashion. This was an interest they shared and there are frequent discussions on fashion and clothes in their correspondence. On this occasion she wrote,

> Now as to dress, a fearful idea weighs upon me. Usually I don't object to new fashions, but I have seen several terrible forebodings lately, of most scanty skirts really as flat behind as before right down to the heels, two of them were long enough to trail 10 inches, only not <u>full</u> enough!! And on evidently frenchy dressy people! not a crease of fullness anywhere, all tight. My velvet will look like a ballet skirt! Another revolution is that as I said, there are not particularly winter hats, the best now are tulle and lace . . .

One visit which made Agnes open her eyes somewhat was to a rather dysfunctional family in Lancashire who seem to have been painting friends of Frank. She wrote to her mother,

> Did you know that the eldest son, a boy of 23, has married the daughter of the dancing mistress Mrs. Wordsworth! They are all miserable about it. The daughter insists on living in London to visit the poor and is attending lectures on the Old Testament but when she is here she refuses to help with the cottagers. Mrs. M. seems very good to the poor here, and has taken me into many cottages, as we pass, and is great friends with all the sick and aged and ill. Then Mr. M. cares for none of them, does not like religion or politics, does not look after his property or anything, only paints all day, and wants to sell this place and live in London by himself in a studio. Mr. and Mrs. quarrel incessantly, in fact are barely on speaking terms – never speak to each other at meals. The son who is here, a smart masher, is wanting to go and join the 11th Hussars but they cant, yet, get the father to allow it. So he hangs about grumbling at the bad fires, or the weak coffee, or spots on the table cloth, and unpunctuality and is a constant worry to his mother. She talks incessantly so that I am very much buttonholed . . .

By the end of 1900 Baden-Powell was the Hero of Mafeking. In October he wrote urging Henrietta and Agnes to visit him in South Africa and offering, as inducements, a maid and £100. Henrietta was away from home when the invitation arrived and wrote to Azzie,

> But I want so to get home to hear your verdict on Stephe's very generous – very full invitation? He providing a Maid for us! And that she should meet us on the steamer too! More than Aunt Constance did for us. And £100 sent on in advance. And for engaging rooms for us! It is all too much. I do not see that any better campaign for you could be devised! To escape the winter when you would be in bed (if in London at home) with colds, and chills. Then return in the spring for London. But if you think well to go to the Cape – we must be prepared to stay a visit at Government House – and you will need at least 2 or 3 more dresses, and we shall have much to settle, and to pack . . . Solely for health, as for Society we shall see much better I trust amongst the Military and governing men at the Cape.

The mention of Aunt Constance presumably refers to another possible visit to Malta.

And so the offer was accepted and the ladies arrived on 17 December, with the intention of staying until April.

While at the Cape Henrietta and Agnes were staying at the same hotel as the sixty-two-year-old Speaker of the South African Parliament, Sir William Bisset Berry. A promising courtship developed. However Agnes was there as the guest of the great Baden-Powell and anything to do with him was News. Although the papers at the time were dominated by an epidemic of cholera, some of them found space to print some malicious gossip about Agnes and Sir William. Henrietta was furious; she had a row with Sir William and marched Agnes straight off home. Although deeply upset about this Agnes, at the age of forty-two, still did not rebel. However, she did write to her mother,

> I do wish you could spare a little of your thought to settle what is to become of me. You all seem to think I had better be a sort of general ADC and I don't call that life.

Agnes and Sir William retained an affection for each other and they continued to correspond. In 1915, when Sir William's grandson joined the Scouts, the Speaker asked his granddaughter Beatrice why she was not a girl scout. When she told him that there were no girl scouts in Queenstown he wrote to Agnes. Beatrice wrote many years later,

> As a result of my Grandfather's letter to Miss Baden-Powell I received a letter from her welcoming me as a Girl Guide . . . I was only ten years old so really not the age for a Girl Guide. We wrote to each other a couple of times a year for several years.
>
> When I was in Std. IV in 1916, I had a remarkable teacher . . . I remember her arousing my interest in drought resisting plants (Xerophytes). I must have made some mention of this in a letter to Miss Baden-Powell. She sent me a book on Elementary Botany, inside of which she glued a New Year greeting card.

In her letter to the little Beatrice von Linsingen Agnes wrote,

> My dear little friend Beatrice, I shall be so pleased to welcome you as a Girl Guide and am sure you will make a splendid one, as you are a grandchild of my dear friend. You will become a Guiding star to those who are lost in the darkness of ignorance and wickedness. I am posting you the Handbook as a little tiny present and would like to know if you like it.
>
> Please give my kindest remembrances to Sir Bisset. I want to know how he is and whether you take good care of him.

When, in 1917, Beatrice was able to become a Guide in the newly formed 1st Queenstown Company and her patrol was told to choose an emblem, Beatrice showed her Patrol Leader her

> Agnes Baden Powell book of the 1st London Patrol's little flag – the Ivy Leaf Patrol. Of course our 1st Queenstown Patrol became the Ivy Leaf Patrol too!

What a lovely step-grandmother Agnes would have made. Sir William died in 1922 and, in 1999, his library was transferred to the Rhodes

University in Queenstown. The breadth of interests shown in his books demonstrates what an admirable husband he would have made for Agnes.

Shortly after Agnes and Henrietta left the Cape, Stephe came home and over a hundred family members celebrated the Hero's return with a lunch for him. The meal comprised ten courses, including coffee. Agnes' social circle widened even further as so many of Stephe's Army friends also came home; of one of them Agnes wrote, '. . . [he] says he just loves dancing with me!' On another occasion, while staying at Codford St Mary in Wiltshire, Agnes wrote, 'We go into the billiard room at night and have grand games of fives, which I was glad to learn.'

In November 1902, shortly before the move to Palace Gate, Agnes was expecting to go on a visit to Sicily. Preparations were obviously thorough as she wrote that [Sir W. Tomlinson] 'thinks there are so many brigands in Sicily we must each buy a revolver, I am to come and practise on the House of Commons Terrace.' Obviously she needed some warmer weather as she wrote at about the same time, 'I cogitate and discuss morning and night whether I had not better go to the Cape, but cannot come to <u>any</u> conclusion.' Certainly she had, on previous occasions, compared the London weather unfavourably with that in the Cape but was she, perhaps, still wrestling with her relationship with Sir William?

Agnes was riding a lot at this time as she was exercising Stephe's ponies prior to them being sold. Throughout this period Henrietta was experiencing a great deal of minor ill health: mouth ulcers, flu and such things which were tactfully handled by her daughter. Nevertheless, Agnes was still able to get away from time to time. Indeed, by this time she was frequently being invited to stay with friends so that she could paint watercolour pictures of their houses. These visits took her far and wide. In September she was in Kelso, in Scotland and then, later in the month, she had moved on to Dunglass from where she wrote,

Bridge is rather dull here, as two of us are left out, and we have no music. At the other five houses I sang a great deal. I have got a nice sketch done of this house, though it is difficult to make it look grand enough.

While visiting Braco she wrote to her mother,

> I have been quite laughing to myself at the keen rivalry between all
> these old gentlemen as to who is to get a walk with me. They have
> each been in turn to engage me, and seem quite anxious to secure the
> fun to themselves.

The following month she was writing with a request that Baden should
get for her a new book, *New Conceptions in Science* by Stein and a
few days later that she was 'learning to crochet a sweet little jacket' for
Francis and Florence's new son, Bobby.

One interesting thing about the family is the probably unique system
of symbols which was used to denote the days of the week. This was
used in letters and memos and within correspondence.

On 27 December 1904 the first performance took place of *Peter Pan*
and the play took fashionable London by storm. Agnes may have been
there; certainly on 15 January, when Warington was sent a ticket, she had
already seen it. However, she went again with Baden on 17 March and
found that Francis and Florence were sitting next to them. In between
those two occasions, Agnes stayed with friends in Wales where the
activities of the house party included hunting, singing, Bridge and round
games. Being the sister of her brothers, Agnes tended to ride with the
men during the hunts, rather than go in the carriages with the ladies.

Towards the end of that month all the brothers seem to have been
at home, or expected there, but Henrietta had gone away for a month.
However, she seemed unable to believe that the house could run
without her for she was fretting to get home. Agnes sent her letters
telling precisely what she had been doing in the management of the
home and encouraging her mother to make the most of the beneficial
effects of her time away. She cleverly suggested little bits of planning
that Henrietta could do while she was away. She reported that someone
had ordered in firewood and sought confirmation that her mother
allowed the cook to order supplies. Two days later she had one of those
days that everybody experiences:

> We have been undergoing the pleasure of a day of the carpenter.
> Baden wanted to have one of my bookcases in his room so, of course

it took a long time for the man to think it over, the wall ornament had to be moved, then he saw to some locks, and my crown, and hung a couple of pictures and all day long I have been up and down after him.

It would seem that they were encouraging Frances to spend more time in London for Agnes goes on to talk of a school in nearby Sloane Street which would do for the young Donald.

ECLIPSE

As we know, Henrietta and the Revd Professor Baden Powell had been drawn to each other partly by their strong shared enthusiasm for science and astronomy, so it was hardly surprising that several of their children should share these interests. The total eclipse of the sun in 1905 occurred just two days before Henrietta's eighty-first birthday, and it must have frustrated her considerably that she was not sufficiently well to go where she could see it properly. However, Agnes and Baden both went to view it, albeit separately.

Agnes was one of a party of 'twenty or more' who cruised the Mediterranean on the P&O Steamer *Arcadia* in order to be in the best possible spot to view the sight. She went in the 'guardianship' of a Sir William. This does not appear, though, to have been Sir William Bisset Berry, but Sir W. E. Tomhusen who was also accompanied by two of his friends, Dr R. P. White and Dr G. E. Chambers. Dr Chambers was an astronomer and played a real part in guiding the others through the experience. The four of them travelled together and appear to have been very good company, the gentlemen all encouraging Agnes to flirt gently with them.

The *Arcadia* sailed from London on 25 August and letters were collected by a pilot boat as they passed the Isle of Wight. The Bay of Biscay was so rough that not only Agnes but even her stewardess were confined to their beds. There were few people on board. Initially Agnes had liked her cabin but it was over the engines and very hot, so the Captain insisted she change it. Sir William was ever attentive and

Agnes and her three companions had lively mealtimes, vacating the dining room long after everybody else. On the day of the eclipse Agnes sent a long, detailed and illustrated letter to her mother, telling her all about it.

I have my little tea party of those I invite every day on deck, no one else seems to have thought of it, and go down below. We ask Dr. Chambers to it because he is so witty and responds to what he calls my 'pleasant asperity' – Sir W. And I have been very busy ruling out charts and he says he is enjoying this trip more than any he can remember. We have also been looking up in Baedeker interesting places to visit in France. I did not go on shore at Gibralter nor did my 'Guardian'. The other ladies got up at 5, and had only had an hour and a half and had to hurry back, though the ship did not start till half past eight. Dr. White bought me a lot of flowers and a basket of fruits which he said were for 'the life and soul of the party' as he calls me. We had such a long wait for the Eclipse to come on, everybody had got into their pet corners and places very soon after breakfast, and the ship was stopped and quite firm and still midway between Majorca and Spain. Some small islands were visible which were most effective during the Eclipse, then the sea became inky black and those rocks [illustrated] stood up like night against a drowning sky, to our North.

However, long before that my Guardian called me to come and have sandwiches and cake at the Buffet all laid out at the Deck House, and there he arranged our two chairs in an unfrequented part of the deck and we brought all our apparatus there, stop watch, camera glasses, binoculars, thermometer (a thing no one else but we had) it went down 5 degrees from 79 in shade to 74, during Totality.

When everything was ready we two went all about to see the other peoples preparations, 4 cats, parrot, and canary Dr White had to report on. 2 men were hoisted to the masthead to see general effects. 2 parties had brought large white sheets, to measure 'shadow bands' on. About 10 were the photograph and Dr Chambers gave me some peeps through his big telescope.

We were in despair when the clouds began to come over thickly, but they cleared off at the right moment, and for over an hour we quietly watched the moon creeping on from a little bit . . . till it covered all and everything looked ashy grey on the ship. I cannot say it was dark nor did the sky look as dark as I had expected, but it was quite like a light night. I busily took my photographs, (which stuck and would not wind off) and then I sketched the corona, and took the thermometer, but it suddenly burst at one point into a flare of light and then very quickly became light again all down the side. These scientifics think that that first flare was a deep cut in the Moon's mountains letting out the light almost sooner than elsewhere – Those who had good enough glasses said the red protuberances were quite splendid but as I had none, I could not see. Dr. Chambers soon came rushing to fetch me to look through his big telescope again, with a dark glass, large sun spots and moon mountains were visible. Oh how tired we were when we got to lunch about 3 pm.

At dinner my Guardian ordered up a bottle of champagne, and toasts were drunk and little speeches made. Then Dr. White proposed my health and made all sorts of compliments saying I was the 'fons et origo' of all that was entertaining and interesting on board. So then Dr. Chambers got up and made good wit of him and said he was sure 'his rival' did not flatter himself he was in my favour, for he knew that I had only been 'twisting Dr. White round her little finger the whole voyage' so this all made a great deal more fun, the Captain put Dr. Chamber's health and then the Captain was thanked and all that. We went out onto the bow of the ship to try to get cool, where a sailor in the dark was singing out about a ship on the starboard bow and other remarks to the man on the Bridge. He caught the sound of my name, and grew enthusiastic at the idea of meeting the General's sister, his brother having been in Mafeking. All our drawings of the corona were ranged in the saloon and Dr. Chambers gave a concluding discourse on the results and thanked everybody.

The following day they disembarked at Marseilles where Agnes and her three friends dined together before Dr White had to go on his way to Paris. Agnes and her escort continued at the Louvre Hotel, as did many other members of their party. Then Sir William was summoned home and Agnes had to be left for the return journey on the *Persia* in the charge of Dr Chambers.

By this time Agnes was growing agitated. She had obviously expected to have a note from Baden, who had watched the eclipse at Nimes, about plans for their return journey. When she did hear from him he told her how he had run into friends, and wanted to return via Constance, and he was running low on cash; did she have any spare that she could send him? In responding to his request she added a PS,

It may interest you to know that some fairly educated people in Poole sat up until Twelve one night watching Mars with the idea that it was one of Major Baden Powell's Balloon operations on Brownsea Island, after observing for three solid hours, as it did not seem to move much or blow up they went to bed.

Agnes returned home on the *Persia*. Shortly afterwards Dr White had one of her Eclipse sketches framed for her.

GUIDES ON THE HORIZON

On 1 August 1907 Baden-Powell held his momentous trial camp on Brownsea Island in Poole Harbour. It seems not to have registered strongly with the family, not surprisingly since they were all used to eccentric activities among themselves. Probably the one for whom the camp registered most was the fatherless young Donald who, at the age of ten, was a last minute addition and the twenty-first member of the camp. It was Donald who was allowed to light the camp fire, with a match, something for which Baden-Powell was roundly told off by Frances.

Later that month Agnes was staying in Hungerford where, as so often happened, she was making pictures of the house, Wormstall. Towards the end of September she was staying with some of her many Parliamentary friends and described herself as being busy with sketching, tennis and motoring. She may have visited the Holy Land at about that time; she certainly sent pressed flowers from there to several people that Christmas.

Shortly after Stephe's return from South Africa, Henrietta and Agnes had been presented at Court. Following this an event occurred which threw the family into overdrive. On 3 October 1909 General Robert Baden-Powell was knighted while visiting the King at Balmoral. Three days later his sister wrote to her mother from 'Baden-Powell Palace', saying that the front door bell never stopped ringing and that she was having to deal with all sorts of issues, apparently including queries from the Press. She again raised the issue of her future:

> I do wish you could spend a little of your thought when you are more rested to settle what is to become of me, because I see that one can very easily be just entirely taken up withal these petty trivialities and make no progress in the long run. It seems to me that you don't grasp this, and you all seem to think I had better be a sort of general ADC and I don't call that life. You must not think that I am complaining, but consider, will it keep me for life – or can you plan any more useful and practical course that will have some result.

Despite Agnes' energy she was suffering from increasing bouts of chest trouble and headaches. In November 1909 she wrote to her mother that she was having to inhale for her chest. However, she was sending her mother two books which reflected their shared interest in women's issues; one was called *Notable Women* and the other was a book about the Women of Scotland in the eighteenth century. The following March she still had the cough and her mother wrote, '... you are much more seriously ill than I am! You have suffered your cough November December January February = 4 full months ...'

Eventually Agnes needed some nursing at home in order to recover. It is noticeable, though, that it was still Henrietta who paid the medical bills. Agnes was 51! And she still had no real role in life.

PART II

The Guiding Years

THE GUIDING YEARS

On 29 September 1909 Sir Robert Baden-Powell held a rally of his Boy Scouts at the Crystal Palace. At the end of the rally there was a march past of the 10,000 Scouts and, at their tail, marched 2,000 girls, dressed in the Scout khaki, complete with all the accoutrements of scarf, haversack, stoh and big hat. When Baden-Powell, feigning ignorance, asked the girls who they were, they announced that they were the 'Girl Scouts'.

This posed a problem for Baden-Powell. He had known for some time of their existence and, in principle, had no objection to girls joining in the great game of Scouting. However, he did realise that to authorise their inclusion would spell death to the burgeoning movement. On the one hand many boys would be put off by the inclusion in their fun of girls and, on the other hand, most parents would not dream of allowing their daughters to become involved in a game in which they were doing adventurous activities alongside boys. These were, after all, the days when single sex education was the norm and girls were heavily chaperoned until they married.

Baden-Powell decided that there should be a separate organisation for the girls. But how should it be run? Scouting had developed naturally; there had been the experimental camp on Brownsea Island in August 1907, followed by the fortnightly issue of *Scouting for Boys* which had taken the country by storm and was already spreading overseas. Baden-Powell approached a couple of the ladies he knew, with a view to one of them taking on the leadership of the girls' organisation, but without success. He then approached Agnes. But she was unwilling: she was already in her fifties, she was leading a full life and, despite her many activities, she was shy and more used to supporting her brothers than taking the lead. Moreover, despite being prominent in public life and Vice-President of the Westminster Red Cross, she did not consider herself as cut out to be a public figure. Some years later her friend, Mrs Benson, would write in the *Girl Guides' Gazette*,

Miss Baden-Powell's idea of a day's work would be a shock to most people. Domestic duties and the care of her aged mother come first, then come the girl guides, and lastly many and varied social duties. Few of the Guides realise how full and busy her life is, and how hard she works for her beloved Guides.

However, Agnes was not unused to young people. She would have come into contact with them in her Red Cross work. In 1908 she started a Boy Scout Troop 'in hopes of finding a man to take it over'. Another venture, also in 1908, was when she mooted the idea of a Girls' Emergency Corps, something which must have been firmly based on Scouting. She wrote, many years later,

We decided to meet on the Green on February 6th, 1909, for the purpose of such formal inauguration as might be decided at this meeting.

This instinctive type of approach to a task was typical of Agnes and would cause her difficulties later on when she was working the 'committee types'.

The suggestion seems always to have been made that Baden-Powell was taken aback by the sight of girls at Crystal Palace. This is not so, for he had been used from his earliest years to boys and girls being together. Although Agnes was the only surviving girl in the family she was the nearest to him in age. They were alike in appearance and in having many gifts. As young children they had been educated together, had played together and, as an adult, Agnes was involved in many of her younger brother Baden's activities. In a family in which all things were held in common, there would be no novelty in the idea of girls borrowing their brothers' copies of *Scouting for Boys* and wishing to join in their Scouting. Indeed, as early as 16 May 1908 Baden-Powell had written in *The Scout*, under the title 'Can girls be Scouts',

I have had several letters lately asking whether scouting would be a good thing for girls to take up, and whether there was any chance of their being sufficiently plucky to make good scouts.

I have replied that I think girls can get just as much healthy fun and as much value out of scouting as boys can.

Some who have taken it up have proved themselves good scouts in a very short time. As to pluck, women and girls can be just as brave as men, and have over and over again proved it in times of danger. But for some reason it is not expected of them, and consequently it is seldom made part of their education, although it ought to be; for courage is not always born in people, but can generally be made by instruction.

At about this time Agnes wrote a pamphlet of the type which girls wishing to be Girl Scouts could show to their parents. It takes the form of a correspondence between a girl, Dorothy, and her parents who have some misgivings about her joining. Agnes said that they are an actual correspondence which passed between parents in India and their daughter at school in England. In her introduction Agnes states her hope that the mother's objections will be met by the institution of the Girl Guides.

From then on there were few editions of *The Scout* that did not carry some reference to the Girl Scouts. Indeed, Baden-Powell was not averse to the formation of mixed patrols of scouts. But he was aware of the need for a separate organisation. In *The Scout* of 16 January 1909 he wrote,

> . . . I have had greetings from many patrols of Girl Scouts, for which I am very grateful. They make me feel very guilty at not having yet found time to devise a scheme of scouting better adapted for them; but I hope to get an early opportunity of starting on it.

The Scout of 10 July 1909 had a long article, under the title 'Is Scouting Good for Girls?', which included instructions about the uniform for Girl Scouts 'a modified gym costume similar to the following: Scarlet biret, haversack, jersey and short skirt, (both dark blue) belt, light staff, stockings (pulled up over the knees).' A note is added to the effect that 'General Baden-Powell is writing a book, "Scouting for Girls" which, I hope, will be ready in the autumn.' Agnes and Henrietta were both so interested in dress that their influence is surely evident in the advice given on uniform and this would seem to have been necessary.

1 Agnes, aged about twenty.

2 A transatlantic postcard
of Agnes.

3 One of Agnes' paintings in Algiers, 1892.

4 A scene in Algiers painted by Agnes, 1892.

Above left: 5 President of the Girl Guides.

Above right: 6 In her uniform of her own design.

7 Agnes' signature.

Africa from Gibraltar   Pearl Rock   Tarifa Pt   AB-P 92

8 One of Agnes' paintings of Gibraltar.

Night. Steaming out of Gibraltar 1892. ABP

9 'Night Steaming out of Gibraltar'. A painting by Agnes, 1892.

Above: 10 Henrietta Baden-Powell in her early widowhood.

Right: 11 The first handbook, published in May 1912.

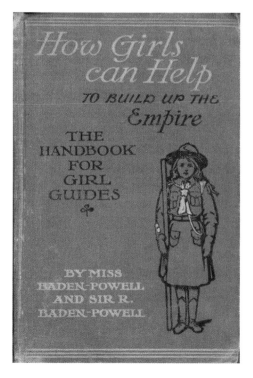

12 A hand-painted postcard sent to a newly appointed commissioner.

Above left: 13 Hard at work.

Above right: 14 The Reverend Baden Powell, Savilian Professor of Geometry at Oxford.

THE BEGINNING

Mrs Henrietta Grace Baden-Powell (1824–1914) and her daughter Agnes (1858–1945). Both women did a tremendous amount to encourage Robert Baden-Powell in his scheme for Girl Guides. Agnes' role of first President and authoress of 'How Girls Can Help To Build Up The Empire' (the first Handbook) is perhaps better known than Henrietta's. B.-P. wrote: 'When I first put forward the idea of the Girl Guide Movement I was not so very hopeful about it myself, until my mother, with her ripe experience and plucky spirit, urged me to go ahead.'

Opposite. The Founder (1857–1941) and Chief Guide (1889–1977) in uniform, in 1931.

15 Agnes and Henrietta, c. 1880.

Mrs. Baden-Powell. Mrs. Baden-Powell is one of the most wonderful old ladies in the kingdom. She has just celebrated her eightieth birthday, surrounded by her devoted children, who gave her a gold toilet-service in honour of the occasion. The gallant defender of Mafeking must have often turned his mind homeward during the anxious weeks and months of that historic siege, for the Baden-Powells are a very united family. On Mafeking Night Mrs. Baden-Powell's house at Knightsbridge was surrounded for hours by an enthusiastic crowd, which must have somewhat, one would suppose, have disturbed the bees whose hive has always been a prominent feature of her London home. Of late years this remarkable octogenarian has taken up astronomy as a hobby, and she spends long hours gazing at the stars.

Royal Doubles. Now that there is so much talk of "doubles," it is worth noting that nearly every well-known personage has a double who, by careful dressing, does his best to keep up the flattering illusion. King Edward has several, but the one with the strongest resemblance lives in the East-End. The Kaiser's double is a tailor, King Oscar of Sweden's an inhabitant of Lyons, the part of the country, by the way, from which the King's grandfather originally came; and King Leopold of Belgium's is a pickpocket, who takes advantage of the likeness to practise his rascality upon smart crowds on public occasions. Leaving the crowned heads, President Loubet, it was shown the other day, has a double in Paris, while President Roosevelt's likeness is a comic singer, who is now being made use of to throw ridicule on the Republican candidate. M. Combes, the French Premier, is the exact likeness of an old General of the Empire, while M. Pelletan, the French Minister of Marine, is doubled by a bookmaker and a cab-driver.

Napoleonic Relics. There is a little town in the South of France which boasts that Napoleon once lived within its walls when he was an ambitious youth. The little house in which the future Emperor stayed, and the modest chamber which was all that his means would permit him to hire, are shown with much pride by the municipality, and visitors to the shrine are conducted to the room by an old soldier, who sees that no irreverent person cuts his name upon the treasured relics. For years past the room and its ancient furniture have attracted visitors to the place, and the authenticity of the shrine has never been questioned. But, unfortunately, the Municipal Council fell out with one of the inhabitants who knew too much, and this man, out of revenge, has made public the fact that the treasured furniture was bought by the Town Council at a second-hand shop in Paris and secretly placed in the room. What is worse, he has conclusively proved his statement, and people now even doubt whether the great Napoleon ever stayed in the town at all.

A Fighting Trappist. The General of the Trappists, that stern order which insists upon absolute silence among its members, has just died in Rome. His name was Sebastien Wyart, and he was a man with a history, for in 1870 he was a Captain of the Pontifical Zouaves and fought all through the Franco-Prussian War. Captain Wyart was the leader of that small band of Zouaves which, on Oct. 11, 1870, was ordered to support and encourage the raw levies of the Cher in trying to stop the march of the Germans on Orleans. With his small body of Zouaves and the Mobiles of the Cher, Captain Wyart took up a position in a wood and for two hours held a Bavarian column which was marching to Orleans. For this exploit he

MRS. BADEN-POWELL (MOTHER OF THE DEFENDER OF MAFEKING), WHO HAS JUST CELEBRATED HER EIGHTIETH BIRTHDAY.

Photograph by Langfier, Old Bond Street, W.

16 Henrietta at eighty.

17 Agnes firing the new Maxim gun at Stoke park.

Right: 18 & 19 The Women's Aerial League meets at Hendon.

Below left: 20 Taking part in a bicycle gymkhana.

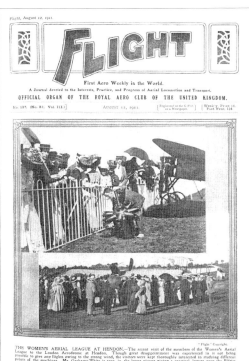

LETTER FROM AGNES BADEN-POWELL

With the help of the French Government a wireless station was established at Wimereux near Boulogne in Northern France, with the intention of transmitting and receiving messages across the Channel. The corresponding station used was at the South Foreland Lighthouse near Dover. After a series of experiments, on the 27th March 1899 messages were successfully transmitted from Wimereux and received across the Channel at South Foreland.
A newspaper of the time, 29th March 1899, reported that;

'Messages passed backwards and forewards with the greatest care and quickness'.

This letter was written by Agnes Baden-Powell to Marconi to congratulate him on this success. The letter reads:

'Will you allow me to congratulate you warmly on the grand success you have achieved, in actually bridging the Chanel, it is a splendid triumph, not withstanding the presence of a group of French sceptics.
My Mother and I will be here for a fortnight and we hope very much that you will allow us the pleasure of seeing you if you should come to Bournemouth, where we can tell you how much we appreciate the wonders you have accomplished, for the progress of science, as with us for the comfort of humanity.
We are looking forward eagerly to making the acquaintance of the coherer in person, and only await your arrival to start on our pilgrimage towards Poole.
When may that delightful excursion take place?'

Background Notes to Wimereux:

A wireless station was set up at Wimereux, near Boulogne on 27 March 1899. The station was used to send messages both ways across the English Channel, transmitting and receiving to the South Foreland Station.

—And His Sister Still Enjoys Life, Too

So that she can cut her birthday cake "above the clouds," Miss Agnes Baden-Powell is to celebrate her 80th birthday on December 16 with a balloon ascent.

She has also arranged a 10-miles

Miss Agnes Baden-Powell touching her toes.

horseback ride, a long swim in an open-air pool, and a night under canvas on a palliasse. If the pool is frozen over, then Miss B.-P. will write her age with her skates on the ice.

Originally this 5ft-and-a-bit sister of the Chief Scout planned to ride from London to Nottingham to her balloon, "but friends thought it might be a little too much for me," she told the *Sunday Dispatch*. "So I shall only ride the last ten miles.

"I shall take my birthday cake up in the balloon so I can cut it above the clouds," she added.

"I wanted to light the candles up there too, but the pilot said 80 candles alight would be dangerous."

How has this compact, sturdy little body kept so supple for nearly 80 years?

"Plenty of exercise, though I've not bothered much with regular physical jerks. But I can still swing my legs over my head and tap the floor with my feet."

Unhampered by her long tweed coat and hat, down on the floor Miss B.-P. went. And houpla! over her head went her strong little legs, and rat-a-tat went her feet on the floor.

A dozen times she did it, like a clockwork toy up and down among the Victorian knick-knacks of her London rooms.

Then we had touching toes, squatting tailor-fashion on the floor, and trunk rotation. "But I don't do exercises nearly regularly enough."

Above left: 21 Correspondence with Marconi.

Above right: 22 Agnes at eighty, from the *Sunday Dispatch*.

23 The Hyde Park rally, 2 June 1920. Mrs Mark Kerr and Princess Mary, followed by Sir Percy Everett and Agnes.

VISIT TO HOSPITAL

Miss Baden-Powell Chats With Patients

GIRL GUIDES of the Wallington and Carshalton Division lined the drive at Queen Mary's Hospital, Carshalton Beeches, when Miss Agnes Baden-Powell, sister of the late B.P., visited the hospital wards on Sunday morning.

A party of the local Boy Scouts were also present to welcome Miss Baden-Powell, who was met by Miss Janet Allen, Divisional Commissioner, and Miss B. Woodger.

At the hospital steps, she was received by the matron, then proceeded to the wards, accompanied by Miss Newton, Assistant Divisional Commissioner. The party visited each of the wards in turn, and chatted with several of the nurses and patients during the tour.

While walking along London-road, Wallington, on Sunday evening, Mrs. Rosa Court, aged 50, slipped and fell on the pavement. She was taken to Croydon General Hospital, where it was found she had sustained fracture of the right leg.

Above and below: 24 & 25 Agnes visits St Mary's Hospital Carshalton, October 1942.

26 Agnes meets some guides in the street.

Our house 32 Princes Gate 1902.

27 32 Princess Gate in 1902 – the family home for a number of years.

28 A Registration Certificate signed by Agnes, 1912.

29 The Enrolment Certificate of a Canadian guide signed by Agnes, *c.* 1915.

Above left: 30 The family grave at Kensal Green cemetery.

Above right: 31 The grandmother clock presented by Agnes to Girl Guide Headquarters and placed in the library.

32 Agnes' repousse work competition mirror.

33 On tour.

34 Lord Barnard's Raby Castle, December 1899.

35 Sir George Douglas' Springwood Park, December 1899.

36 A painting of Gillingham, 1903.

It has been said that, at this time, the Girl Scouts were competing with each other to wear the hats with the widest brims and carrying the longest staves, usually made from broom handles. Thus it will be appreciated that the 2,000 girls who paraded at Crystal Palace on 4 September, according to the report in *The Times*, were loudly cheered . . . were but the tip of the iceberg. By October 1909, 6,000 Girl Scouts were registered at Headquarters.

In the November Baden-Powell received the following pathetic letter: 'Dear Sir, If a girl is not allowed to run, or even to hurry, to swim, ride a bike, or raise her arms above her head. Can she become a Scout?' Later it became apparent that Guiding was not reaching all girls when a letter in similar vein, but from another part of the social spectrum, was printed in *Home Notes*. A young factory worker wrote to Agnes: 'They provide cricket and football for the boys, but they don't give us girls any amusements.' Agnes went on to comment,

> What do girls do with themselves after hours, or after their long day's work? We have thousands of young girls working in factories – making matches, packing drugs and chemicals, spending long hours turning a handle of a machine, or lifting piles of paper off one engine on to another, amid the din and roar of the machinery.
>
> And at the end of her day's toil what is the state of the girl's mind? Somewhat like a slate with all the writing smudged out. Wait till the clock strikes, and then there pours forth into the streets a living stream of thousands of girls; and where do they go? They should go home, I am told. But they don't go home! Who can induce them to go home, for what is 'home'? Some one stuffy room where mother is perhaps trying to get the washing ironed, with crying babies fidgeting around, or with a drunken father, cross and noisy, and surroundings that are not calculated to bring out the best side of human nature.
>
> Now outdoor interests and hobbies are equally necessary to healthy girlhood as to healthy boyhood.

It was to give Guiding to girls such as these that the YWCA and the Girls' Friendly Society started their own sections of the movement.

Baden-Powell's view was clear, as at this time he was writing, 'If she is to be equally efficient with her brother for work in the world, a woman must be given equal chances with him.' The Girl Guides was obviously overdue and, equally obviously, despite her misgivings, Agnes was seen to be the person to lead it.

In the *Headquarters Gazette* of November 1909 Baden-Powell set out 'The Scheme for Girl Guides'. It included a *raison d'etre* and advice on the way to set it up locally, starting with a local committee who would choose 'suitable' leaders and it displayed none of the spontaneity which accompanied the start of the Boy Scouts when groups of boys would form themselves into patrols and then approach their choice of adult leader, as had also been evident in the formation of the first Girl Scout patrols. The uniform instructions enlarged on the advice given in July by including items such as a billy-can, lanyard and knife, a cape hooked up at the back and a shoulder knot of the group colour. A straw hat was offered as a summer alternative to the scarlet beret and the jumper was to be in the group colour. The straw hat was to be abandoned after a rally when all the hats were ruined in a downpour. The badge system included Second Class, First Class and twenty proficiency badges, the syllabi of several of which referred to that for the Boy Scouts. Seventeen stipulated badges had to be earned for the holder to be admitted to the Order of the Silver Fish, the highest award. The similarity between the Scout and Guide syllabi was to endure until the late 1960s.

By January 1910 plans were well underway for the formation of the Girl Guides with Agnes' involvement. On 25 April she wrote a letter to Audrey Lloyd of Norwich who had just registered as a Guide. The first Company to be registered was in Norwich, under the Captaincy of Miss A. del Riego. It was the 1st Pinkney's Green Company (Miss Baden-Powell's Own).

Agnes began to think about the practicalities of the new project. On 8 April she met with two friends, Mrs William Paget and Mrs Hayes-Sadler, to consider renting an office and to engage a paid secretary. Even with a secretary Agnes seemed to write all her letters by hand. A month later, on 2 May, an Advisory Committee was formed and Agnes was elected President. However, it was not until 21 January 1911 that the first drawing room meeting, to interest influential people, was held at No.18 Park Lane. At this meeting the principal speaker was Baden-

Powell and those who had been invited included the wives of Lords Lieutenant.

By May 1910 a Committee had been established. A meeting on the second of that month, under the chairmanship of Mrs Alan Gardner, and attended by Agnes as President, heard a progress report from Miss del Riego. Few of those who attended were to remain involved for long, although Miss Macdonald, the Secretary, was to give long and loyal service until her resignation in 1919. Initially she received £2 10s per week, which comprised a salary of £1 15s and 15s for office expenses. Agnes had obviously selected her committee members carefully, for each of those present had a designated task relating to her skills and contacts. It is evident from the minutes that despite the family's shortage of cash, Agnes was underwriting the burgeoning movement. She had found an office at No.116 Victoria Street and had temporarily guaranteed the rent. She had also paid for a stock of badges which she had had supplied – unfortunately this generosity was to cause her problems later. On 31 May Baden-Powell and Agnes formally announced the formation of the Girl Guides.

It would seem that Agnes did not anticipate that the Guides would take up a vast amount of her time for there is little sign from her correspondence that her travels abated significantly. There is often no mention at all of the Guides in her letters home. One place she did visit frequently, and which was significant in Guiding, was Cambridge. She was a friend of the de Beaumonts, a mother and daughter who were to play a substantial part in Guiding in that county. Letters Agnes wrote to her mother during visits to Cambridge in 1910 and 1911, when she appears to have stayed with a University family at Westroad Corner, give an impression of much business; with the encouragement of new Guide companies, interspersed with worship in the college chapel and a great deal of socialising. As seemed to happen whenever she was away from home, she was constantly agonising over whether to accept invitations to stay on longer or to go on to another family. By this time Henrietta was eighty-six and Agnes had effectively taken on the main burden of the housekeeping, although she never failed to do it in consultation with her mother. Indeed, much of the content of her letters is about such household matters as whether more meat is needed from the butcher and the care of clothes. One could surmise that Agnes could never have taken on the responsibility of being an active President of the Girl Guides if the family had not the support of their excellent cook/housekeeper and maid.

With the new scheme successfully having been launched, the Committee realised that, like their brother Scouts, the Guides needed some organ of communication. They approached Pearson's, who did the Scouts' publishing and whose Percy Everett was, and remained, an important person in the development of Scouting. It was agreed that, from 11 August, the Girl Guides should have two pages each week in *Home Notes*, a ladies' magazine. In each edition these pages would start with an invigorating piece from Agnes, which would be followed by brief items carrying news of companies' activities, information about tests, advice on the activities that Guides could undertake, and there was the continuing discussion, which went in parallel with that in the Committee, about the uniform. Guides were ever thus.

At the start of the first pages in *Home Notes*, on 11 August, 1910, Agnes wrote,

> Dear Girl Guides,
> How I wish I could see you all, but as you are so scattered over the Empire, shall we communicate with each other in this paper? 'Home Notes' will reach you all, however far away – South Africa or Australia or wherever you are. I shall be so pleased to hear what you are doing, and hope to get news of you.

Other items in that edition included 'Information as to joining the Baden-Powell Girl Guides' and 'Cookery for Girls'. Each week there were helpful articles explaining the basics of Girl Guiding; interestingly it was not until 18 October that one appeared about the Guide Law.

On 25 August Agnes was still writing in a rather tentative vein, referring to Guiding as 'an experiment' and stressing the womanly side of its purpose. By 17 November she was writing much more vigorously, almost in the sense of 'up girls and at 'em', with strong words about character training and earning the money they needed. It would seem that the distribution of *Home Notes* was not confined to Britain, since the pages included queries and reports from some overseas countries, especially in the Empire, as it was still known. Agnes, as an artist, was taking a detailed interest in the layout of the Guide pages. In a letter written to her mother from Lindis on 29 August, in which she talks about what she has been eating, of having received things sent from home (usually on the next day), her inability to send any more honey and her distress at learning of children working in mines (she does not say where, for it was, by then, illegal in Britain) there is a paragraph which reads,

> I enclose the 'Home Notes' articles, 3 numbers, but am not very pleased with the look of them. Miss Middleton (Editress) has chosen such poor illustrations and has mixed up other people's paragraphs in my letters.

By the end of 1910 Guiding was established. It had grown with a little more organisation than had Scouting, using as a basis the scheme set out by Baden-Powell at the end of the previous year. However, within those parameters, each company was more or less doing its own thing. The Committee realised that clearer guidelines were needed – Agnes had her next task. Her response was to produce a threepenny leaflet called *Pamphlet A*. This set out the rules of Guiding and Rose Kerr, writing in 1932, stated that there was no rule in it which would need to be rescinded in the very well-established Guiding of that time.

The battle was still being waged, and would be for some time, over whether Guiding was a suitable activity for girls. Another pamphlet was needed from Agnes. *Pamphlet B*, also at the price of threepence, was a promotional leaflet, the sort of thing a girl could take home to her parents to explain the fascination of Guiding. It starts off,

> Girls! Imagine that a battle has taken place in and around your town or village . . . what are you going to do? Are you going to sit down, and wring your hands and cry, or are you going to be plucky, and go out and do something to help . . .

What followed was similar in spirit to what Baden-Powell had written in *Scouting for Boys* in that it encouraged the girls to 'be prepared' for all emergencies and discussed ways in which this could be achieved.

The recognition of those girls was established early on with an award scheme. Awards were sent out with a very personal letter, written by

Agnes. One who rose to such emergencies, accompanying a Badge of Merit on 23 October 1911, reads,

> My dear Guide Nibby,
> I was so very pleased to hear of your brave conduct in so promptly saving the life of the drowning boy, as well as that of your companion. I most heartily congratulate you on your bravery, and we can hold you up as an example to everybody as having been 'prepared'.

Five years later she was writing,

> My dear Patrol Leader,
> I have great pleasure in sending you the Girl Guides Silver Cross awarded for Bravery, as I think you have thoroughly deserved it. I am so glad you did not hesitate to go quickly to the rescue of your companion and I congratulate you on Being Prepared, being able to swim and doing you duty. How nice it is you have the Bronze Medal too.

It is noticeable that Agnes paid each of the girls the courtesy of not addressing them by their Christian name.

By the time the Girl Guides was up and running Baden-Powell was living at home in Princes Gate. Agnes had always mixed with the intelligentsia in Society and her circle of friends and acquaintances was widened even further by her brother's presence. In May 1911 he met Juliette Gordon Low, the remarkable woman who was taking Girl Scouting to America. They had a great deal in common and Stephe brought Juliette home to tea where she discovered that she also shared many interests with Agnes. On that occasion she particularly enjoyed looking at Agnes' nature collections.

Agnes was also writing for a different publisher. After a year of having two pages in *Home Notes* the Committee decided that this agreement should cease. Since the contract had begun there had been some opposition, especially from Mrs Agatha Blyth. This may have been because the Guide contribution seemed somewhat incongruous, sitting as it did among articles such as advice to the lovelorn. Percy Everett offered to start a publication especially for the Girl Guides but the suggestion made the Committee nervous. Everett continued to publish the Guide pages in *Home Notes*, free of charge. However, in July 1911 the space available was cut to one page and payment for the articles ceased. In November 1911 the Guides regained their two pages when they moved their contract to a magazine called *The Golden Rule* which may have had a wider general appeal. It also offered a very generous settlement. This arrangement, despite the misgivings of some owing to the denominational nature of the paper, would continue until the *Girl Guide Gazette* was started two years later.

'HOW GIRLS CAN HELP...'

The major Guiding burden on Agnes at this time was the writing of the first proper handbook for Girl Guides which was called *How Girls Can Help to Build up the Empire*. It was written in consultation with Baden-Powell and had incorporated into it large chunks based on *Scouting for Boys*, which Agnes interspersed with chapters on homecraft and womanly activities, not to mention nature study. In later years Olave was to refer to it, with some justification, as the 'little blue muddly'. Much of what Agnes wrote in the book seems rather quaint to us today; nevertheless, it is a remarkable book for its time and would have done much to reconcile some of the more reluctant parents to the great game of Guiding, as well as instilling the spirit of adventure in their daughters. In her September letter to the Guides she was wisely missing no opportunity to plug the book.

Agnes had obviously been overworking and was feeling very unwell. In order to work undisturbed by the responsibilities of housekeeping she took herself away to a guest house called Lindis in Woodhall Spa, Lincolnshire, where she planned to take the waters. The house was run by the Misses Hopps who seem to have been very caring. Agnes stayed in one of the principal rooms, a room over the sitting room, with a bay window, where she was extremely comfortable and had the space and peace that she needed in order to write. She also wrote to her mother, 'I still retain possession of the Porch, which is quite a fresh-air cure, as I can write there sheltered from rain or sun.'

Because she felt so unwell, she stayed at Lindis throughout August and September, under the care of a doctor but making slow progress medically. This, of course, also meant that progress on the book was restricted. She seems not, certainly at this time, to have discovered a name for her illness, although it sounds very like migraine since she was suffering from many headaches and much sickness. She appears to have been convinced that it was something to do with her liver; the doctor, however, seems to have been quite taciturn and only ever advised her to go on drinking and bathing in the waters.

Finance was a continual concern to her at this time. Her mother sent her a cheque which she was loath to accept, and it went backwards and forwards a couple of times before she agreed to keep it. Money was being used fast:

> I am sorry to say the whole amount spent, over 4 weeks, is £13.3s.6d. However there is the return ticket paid 8/- !!! The bath is 2/4 each time. I am sure I don't take that amount of milk or butter, I have been much too sick for that – I thought it best not to say a word, as they seem such nice people and let them know what they can get. Still it is alarming. I always have 1 egg at breakfast and generally a custard or pudding and 11 eggs cost 1/-. Milk is 1 1/2d a pint, 3d a quart.

The baths, which the doctor advised her to take twice a day, at a cost of 2s 4d a time, strikes one as quite expensive when compared with the cost of food; however, she had found a less fashionable source than the Pump Room where she could drink the waters for 3d instead of 6d – and it was nearer. Other commodities which Agnes considered to be luxuries included a paper of pins at 1d, red flannel socks at 1d and, for the same price, some blotting paper.

Besides the cheque which she eventually accepted from her mother, Agnes was understandably delighted to receive an Income Tax refund of £5 15s. She might have been receiving other small amounts of income. In August a cheque arrived for 4 guineas for her article in *Home Notes*. Although she writes 'article' in the singular she was, of course, making a regular contribution and the four guineas could have been a weekly source of income. These sums, however, did not go into her budget but into that of the Girl Guides. A month later there would be income, too, from the book as she writes that three publishers were eager to take it and that Pearson's had offered £250 down and 15 per cent on sales. These sums, also, would go into Guide funds.

Agnes had her little dog Pepin with her at Lindis, and one has the impression that her daily correspondence with her mother gave her a contact with home which she needed. Half way through her time there she pressed her mother to come for a stay but this apparently came to nothing. Throughout her time at Woodhall Agnes was asking whether Stephe was yet home as she was so anxious to consult him about the book. The book was eventually completed and, on 7 February 1912, all the members present at the Committee meeting signed a paper authorising it to be the only official handbook. It was published on 10 May that year.

CHANGE IN THE AIR

\On 3 January 1912 Baden-Powell set sail for America on the *Arcadian*. George's children, Donald and Maud, probably accompanied by their beloved Aunt Azzie, waved him off at Southampton. Nobody could have dreamed what a momentous voyage this would be for the whole family. On the first night out, at the Captain's table, Baden-Powell was sat next to a Harold Soames of Dorset who was accompanied by his twenty-two-year-old daughter, Olave. When Baden-Powell saw her walking on deck he recognised her as a girl whose gait had impressed him when he had walked behind her in Hyde Park two years previously. Ship-board romances are notoriously fickle but this one was to last. It is generally assumed that, by the end of the voyage, Baden-Powell was thinking seriously about marriage and discussing with Olave the very real problems which stood in their way. For a start he was over thirty years her senior. Also the contribution he made to the family income from his Army pension was essential to the family exchequer. The necessary deliberations were to last for some months. Fortunately Baden-Powell was at the start of a journey round the world on Scout business, so they both had time to think over the matter. However, there is some reason to believe that, by the time of his return, Baden-

Powell may have expected that Olave would have thought better of an alliance which involved such a great disparity in age. On his return to England he immediately took the fatherless Donald on a promised trip to Norway, without communicating with the Soames family, and it was not until Mr Soames contacted him that he resumed his relationship with the family.

In April of that year Agnes was staying in Stratford-on-Avon where she attended a Boy Scout rally which was heralded by bugles. It is quite clear that, by this time, she was already drawing back from the committee work of the Guides. As so often happens a while after the start of a new organisation the personnel on the committee had changed and it is possible that Agnes felt less comfortable working with the new members. It is quite certain that committee work was not a milieu in which this actively practical woman felt at home. In the April meeting issues had been discussed about the salute and the designation of officers, both of which were considered to need her decision. However, it is quite apparent that, should the Committee disagree with Agnes' view, they were quite prepared to follow their own line regardless. It was at this time that the Guides took a room, at the rent of £35 per annum, in the Scout Headquarters.

In the November of 1911 a number of Vice Presidents had been appointed and, by May 1912, Agnes was requesting a meeting of Vice Presidents 'and others'. The one comment which the Committee minuted was that it would be an opportunity to read the Annual Report to those interested. Their overriding concern at this time was the public image of the Guides, especially in relation to public appearances about which, on the whole, they were not very happy. It was still, after all, an uphill struggle to convince careful parents that Guiding was suitable for their daughters. The following month the Committee referred to Agnes the even bigger problem of complaints about Guides marching with Scouts. Plans for the reception went ahead and, by the following month, the questions of singers and speakers for it were being discussed.

Towards the end of July Agnes was staying in Frant in Sussex. There were two Guides in Sunday's lunch party and, afterwards, they all drove over to look at the Boy Scouts' 'farm'. Agnes wrote to her mother that, 'I felt so frightened I could not do much'. However, she obviously did something right as she was immediately asked to pay a similar visit to some nearby Girl Guides on the following day, thus prolonging her stay.

Agnes' interest in air travel was uppermost a couple of weeks later when she was staying in Cowes for Cowes Week. She wrote to Warington, the brother who had been a sailor, of the motor-water-planes which were exciting such interest as they, 'whizz about among the yachts, throwing up wash waves, and then rise up, and fly away over the estuary and back in no time'.

On her way home she stayed in Alresford, having 'left Cowes very empty and dull and wet'. When she arrived the Girl Guides were drawn up at the hall door, in uniform, all ready to salute her. Advantage was taken of her presence to invite her to present the Challenge Cup for ambulance work, of which the Alresford Guides were the first recipients.

In mid-September Baden-Powell dropped the bombshell of his engagement to Olave Soames when he wrote to his mother, telling her that he had been wondering what to give her for her birthday and offering her a potential daughter-in-law. On 18 September he took her to meet his mother for the first time.

In later years Olave was to be quite disparaging about Agnes, suggesting that Baden-Powell's sister resented and looked down on her, but Agnes' writings suggest anything but that. It seems more likely that the young Olave lacked self-confidence and felt quite out of her depth among the sophisticated Baden-Powells. She had had a difficult childhood, being very close to her father but distanced from her mother who made no secret of her preference for her elder daughter, making Olave feel ugly and inadequate. Her closest friend was a woman, considerably older than herself, who had come into her life when she was about ten. This lady, known as Ba, was as energetic and good at sport as was Olave, and she dressed in tweeds with a collar and tie and webbing puttees. Femininity Olave associated with her mother and she must have felt threatened in the very feminine atmosphere of No. 32 Prince's Gate. The date for the wedding was fixed just six weeks ahead.

There is nothing in Agnes' letters during that period to suggest that her brother's engagement had made much impact on her. It could be that she was so stunned that the only way she could cope was by carrying on as usual. In mid-October she was in Petersfield and Stockbridge on what she referred to as 'a little spree', inspecting Guides and attending several rallies. The only thing in her letters that could possibly refer to Olave is an enquiry as to how her mother was after 'the big family party', presumably an engagement party. A week later she is firmly at her Guide work when she sends out an award for bravery, something which appears to have been in her gift.

Olave's sister, Auriol, had had a large wedding just a year previously. In contrast Stephe's wedding, which took place on Sunday, 30 October 1912, was a quiet affair, only fifteen people being present. The bride, who was dressed in pale blue, was attended by Agnes, who was also one of the witnesses, as was Baden who was the Best Man. These two were the only members of the family who were able to be present. The event had not started auspiciously, as Agnes wrote to her mother from the Canford Cliffs Hotel in Bournemouth,

I found no fly at the station but got a miraculous one, then had to order a fly by telephone and chose a room 5/-. He crept like a snail, with his <u>drag</u> on! And at last landed me at Grey Rigg [the Soames' home] where the manservant said '<u>not at home</u>'. However, on hearing my name, he nearly had a fit of capers, and showed me in. Olave ran out to kiss me with delight, Mrs. Soames in a white satin tea gown, and Miss Bower [Ba] were in the drawing room, that was all. Tea was brought and then afterwards Olave carried me off to see her room, and all the pictures and the pretty house, and we sat and had a long chat in the Music Room. Finally I got into my fly and came back here in torrents and storms of rain. It all went off very nicely and pleasantly and they gave me full directions where to go tomorrow. Sir Robert and Mr. H. Soames will come then from Montacute and Mr. Davidson, but the sister has had a sudden attack of gastric chill and is in bed with fomentations. Mrs. Soames will go to her directly after the wedding. No attempt at asking us to the house!! A compartment and lunch has been reserved for the couple. I was sorry to leave you alone and would have been happier if you were in the hands of a doctor. You must hold your jubilation at 12.30 in London . . . and drink their health at lunch. They will arrive at 3.30.

From this it will be seen that Agnes really was prepared to go more than half way to welcome her new sister-in-law into the family, albeit the family may have had reservations either about the wedding or about the Soames family.

When the Girl Guides' Committee met on 6 November, a letter was read out from Agnes expressing her apologies that she was unable to attend meetings because of the large amount of work which devolved upon her as President. Some idea of what this work involved is given by other items in the minutes. For instance it was planned that she should make a tour of inspection in the north of England and Scotland. The minutes tell us that the Committee discussed the question of allowing Agnes the necessary travelling expenses but deferred a decision until the next meeting because the funds were urgently needed for other things. Because of this it was decided that an appeal letter should be written to the *Daily Mail*, signed by Agnes and others.

The previous month Agnes, who was in favour, and the Committee had disagreed on whether Guides should be allowed to parade with Scouts. The question had been settled by Baden-Powell who had recently inspected the two movements on the same occasion. Nevertheless, the Committee continued to believe that Girl Guides should never be allowed to train with Boy Scouts or to march with them.

At the same meeting it was agreed that Agnes should be paid her train fare for the forthcoming visit to the north and Scotland and 'laid down as a standing order that, if any of the Headquarters staff were asked to speak at a meeting out of London, their railway fare should always be offered them'. However, as on this occasion the purpose of Agnes' journey was to encourage Guiding in Scotland, the Scottish Committee was to be asked whether it was prepared to pay her return fare. One can gain a very accurate idea of what was involved in these visits from a letter which she wrote to her mother from Manchester when she was on her way north.

We had a grand show of Girl Guides and the Boy Scouts' band attended too. They drilled and did ambulance bandaging beautifully, we sitting on the dais. I was presented with a bouquet and was asked to address them. There was a great deal of cheering, and finally the Guides and Scouts lined the path of the carriageway from the school and gave wild hurrahs, and the boys trumpeted and drummed. I think it was a deep satisfaction to Mr. Heywood, and he does a great deal to help on both the Corps. As he told me how much he valued Miss Astler I bought a beautiful compass and presented it.

An interesting insight into the life of the time is conveyed in the added information that the butler had been glad to be offered the cost of Agnes' cab fare which he had himself paid.

By 1913 the Girl Guides was an established and growing movement. On 7 January the *Court Circular*, to which Agnes was no stranger, heralded that on the following day the Girl Guides were to hold a special rally at Olympia when Agnes would inspect their camp and present the colours.

By the end of the month she was again in the north and on her way to Scotland. The trip seems to have been mainly for the purpose of doing Guide work, including a deal of writing, and Agnes seems to have needed to tread a diplomatic path between numerous invitations to visit, or stay with, various people and her need of the necessary quiet in which to work. Her first stop was in Richmond, in Yorkshire, from where she visited a very successful and pleasant Rally in Darlington. As well as the ubiquitous ambulance drill, the Guides demonstrated signalling and Agnes was asked to judge the rolls, cakes and petit four which the Guides had made. Several towns had taken part and Agnes wrote to her mother that, 'It was most difficult to award the prizes as Darlington was so very good at all – and I did not want Darlington to have all the prizes.' She then joined the ladies for tea while the Guides ate up the cakes in another hall.

The next stop for Agnes was Edinburgh. She was sent on her way by her kind hosts in Richmond, armed with additional warm clothes to face the atrocious weather and a list of ladies in Scotland who were likely to prove sympathetic to the Girl Guides. In Edinburgh she received another very warm welcome and discovered that she was expected to attend up to three meetings a day, usually taking the Chair. After three years at the head of the Girl Guides this shy woman confided to her mother that 'The whole thing has gone 'without an itch' – except that I feel so awkward at speaking.' To those accustomed to attending Guide events in uniform, it is interesting to note that

Agnes attended an evening uniformed, rally wearing an evening dress and a black cloak. An unconventional approach to uniform was to be evident in later years.

As usual Agnes remained firmly in touch with home affairs while she was away. She was glad to know that her mother had had the curtains and blankets cleaned. These, presumably, were the summer ones as she goes on to ask if, 'you have got all the pretty things ready to wear and put out in March?' Also at this time, she heard that Miss Macdonald had resigned as secretary to the Girl Guides but had been persuaded to stay on. This was a manifestation of a problem that was developing within the Guide secretariat.

So on to Stirling, where Agnes stayed with Juliette Low in her Scottish home. She describes her as, 'so fidgety – always writing telegrams – she has applications from 67 places to start Girl Guides in America.' The whole trip seems to have been a triumphal progress, with Agnes receiving invitations from all sides to dine, or stay, with people and with the various Guide events showing increasing numbers. However, by the time Agnes reached Glasgow the pace was beginning to take its toll, so that she wrote to her mother, 'It has been rather close work, what with packing up, and travelling and doing the polite at each fresh house.'

Within a week Agnes had resolved the problem of the demands on her time by taking herself off to Cranston's Waverley Temperance Hotel in Sauchiehall Street, where she considered that the peace was better for her than the socialising which would accompany her acceptance of any of the many offers of hospitality that she had received. She kept her mother up-to-date with her work as she explained,

> I found it too distracting at peoples' houses to get any writing done, as it seemed to be always time to dress for the next meal and be down, <u>in a second</u>.
>
> Here I have a very nice large double bedroom, a drawing room and all – all to myself and can be as late or as early as necessary. Now I have worked off a lot of business for 'The Golden Rule' and Macdonald, and have gone through Mrs. Low's American proofs, but there seems still to be a packet of them waiting, also a roll of Captain's Warrants.

These last because they were awaiting her signature.

Nevertheless, the invitations continued to arrive and some of them had to be accepted. One which she found it necessary to decline with great regret was the offer of some hunting. Before embarking on the trip Agnes had expressed her anticipation of being able to fit in some hunting and she was obviously disappointed to have to decline the invitation.

One request she could have done without was that she should ask her brother to present some people at Court, 'for payment'. She made it quite clear that it was no use asking because he, and the rest of the family, objected to this practice on principle.

On 18 February Agnes' comments to her mother on her sadness on learning of the death of Captain Scott, whom she had met. Faced with the inevitable decision of what was the correct thing to do, she decided that it was no use writing on such an occasion.

Agnes had thoroughly enjoyed her trip to the very frozen north and based her next inspirational article for *The Golden Rule* (the one written in Glasgow?) on it. She concluded by saying that the Guides in Scotland were winning all hearts by their spirited singing of the Girl Guide songs. Singing was a subject on which there was increasing advice in *The Golden Rule* pages.

At about this time the signs of insufficient liaison between Agnes and the Executive Committee were becoming apparent. Towards the end of February the Committee minuted a decision that Guides should be forbidden to sleep overnight under canvas because of the danger to their health. Yet Agnes had been camping since girlhood and would continue to do so into her eighties. By the following meeting the Committee had received from Agnes a letter on this matter which had obviously caused her a degree of annoyance. However, in the March edition of *The Golden Rule*, the Committee's veto is printed and Agnes' letter remains on the safe subjects of animals and flowers. What went on behind the scenes? On 1 April the Committee passed the resolution 'That as the President is unable to attend the Executive Committee Meetings, the Committee has resolved with much regret to resign office, as it cannot continue to work without her presence.'

One can safely assume that the members of the Executive Committee were women who were, at least, comfortably off, since they had been invited to serve because they had influence. The Baden-Powells, on the other hand, had for the past fifty years bluffed the world into believing that they were in similar comfortable circumstances, whilst living almost from hand to mouth. Agnes' request, prior to her travels, for payment of expenses would have been unusual in a voluntary movement at that time. This, linked with the shoe-string on which the Guides were working, was the cause of the near consternation at her request. Upon her return from Scotland the Committee was dithering over her expenses, possibly requesting more detail than she was able to give, and chasing the various committees whom Agnes had met for their contributions. In addition, the Committee directed that Agnes could not use personal secretarial help (already employed?) but must rely on that available at Headquarters.

The Committee listed for 1913 numbered sixteen members, yet there seems never to have been more than a 50 per cent attendance. By the summer the redoubtable Mrs Lumley Holland had become the Chairman and, from then on, attendance seems to have dwindled even further, being between four and six, including Miss Macdonald, the paid Secretary. The other notable member at this time was Miss Dashwood who represented the YWCA.

Notwithstanding the acute lack of cash the Committee was almost forced, in the summer, to reach the decision to end its contract with *The Golden Rule* and bring out a Guide magazine from January. The reason was that some local Guiders were planning to do so on their own account and this was considered to be unacceptable. However, the Committee was helped in its decision by the offer of £100 from a lady in Brondesbury. This caused further difficulties between Agnes and the Committee. Towards the end of September Agnes wrote to the Committee dissociating herself from any pecuniary involvement in the publication, which she had not advised. The Committee responded in similar terms, pointing out that it had been forced to take the step to pre-empt a similar move from among the membership. At the same time it was decided that the President should be asked to choose the design for the magazine from among the drawings submitted.

Following this meeting Lady Maud Wilbraham, one of the Committee members, had a meeting with Agnes, as a result of which Agnes wrote her a letter saying that, although she had thought it would be a great expense, she believed that the Committee should carry through the scheme. Nevertheless, a week later she was again requesting that the Committee sign a confirmation that she would not be held financially responsible. The Committee responded that, in view of the earlier correspondence, the matter was now considered closed. At the same time, however, the Committee was looking to the Guide President to sign the letter announcing the new publication.

Agnes had other preoccupations at this time. Towards the end of October her brother George's widow, Frances died from kidney failure, having been ill for several years, leaving Maud and Donald orphaned. Maud was by this time eighteen years old, and Donald was two years younger. They made their home in the north with relatives of their mother, although frequent visits were paid to Princes Gate. Of more immediate concern to the Baden-Powells was the loss of the generous quarterly allowance which Frances, the one wealthy member of the family, had made to Henrietta. Frances' funeral took place on Baden-Powell's first wedding anniversary, the day when his and Olave's first child, Peter, was born. At this time Olave was concentrating on being Baden-Powell's wife and, whenever asked about the Girl Guides, would respond that, naturally, her chief work and interest centred on the boys' Movement.

The *Girl Guides' Gazette* was duly launched in January 1914 and at the front of the second, February, issue there was a delightful, if somewhat fulsome, profile of Agnes, written by Mrs E. Benson, a founder member of the Committee who had known Agnes for a long time. In it she suggested that Agnes had been training for the whole of her life for the position which she now held as head of the Girl Guides. She mentioned the eleven languages which her friend spoke; her proficiency upon the organ, violin and piano; her ability as artist, metal worker, writer and needlewoman; and her interest in astronomy, the sciences and nature study. Mrs Benson went on to list Agnes' participation in cycling, swimming, driving and skating; her nursing, cookery and housekeeping skills; the hive of bees in her sitting room, the colony of birds in her hall and her collection of live butterflies. To have such a polymath at the helm of the early Guides must have set the tone for the future. Could it have been a prevailing influence when a new programme, introduced in 1968, was based on eight points, or areas of achievement, which would help to create a fully rounded person? However, there may also be, within the tone of the article, an awareness that Agnes was beginning to come under siege from the Committee, and its Chairman in particular.

By this time Baden-Powell had realised that all was not as it should be on the Executive Committee and he decided to take a hand in its reorganisation. Each member of the Committee would carry a specific responsibility and the status of the Presidency would change. The membership of the Committee was now down to seven plus Agnes and those who were her long-term friends were gradually withdrawing from it. There was a row which went on over several months about the nature of the Presidency, and in this the Committee appeared to be driving Agnes into a corner. In the end the status of the President was reduced to that of a general inspector, acting under the command of the Committee. It was also made clear that expenses would be paid only for trips authorised by the Committee and that the President was debarred from entering into any official correspondence. It is quite evident that the Committee was determined that Agnes should no longer have any authority. When war broke out on 4 August 1914 the exhortation sent to Guide Companies, although nominally signed in printed capitals by Agnes on behalf of the Committee, was in fact signed by Mrs Lumley Holland. Indeed it was only Mrs Lumley Holland who signed the list of suggestions for service which was sent to all the Guides.

By mid-August Agnes had got away from it all and was part of a house party at the home of some friends of Baden's in Hampshire. Although she was there in a purely social capacity, the Guides were not forgotten and she was taken by her hostess to preside at a display and to visit some Guides in camp. It seems that the weather was far from being perfect for camping.

Henrietta was now increasingly frail, Frances' allowance had ceased and Agnes must have been concerned about her own financial future. Henrietta's financial acumen had depended on amassing a succession of various leases and, the year before Frances' death, she had written, 'The only two possessions we have are the two leases of 32, Princes Gate Mews and 9, Hyde Park Gate.' The Princes Gate Mews property included seven stables which gave access to additional income.

Towards the end of July Baden-Powell wrote to Agnes about an annuity which he hoped to provide for her. It had been his intention to provide Agnes with an assured income of £75 a year; sadly, he discovered that this would involve an initial outlay of £1,000 which he could not afford. He arranged, therefore, to pay Agnes a quarterly allowance of £18 15s which, would create an annual total of £75, and to leave her in his will a sufficient sum to purchase an annuity for her future.

By mid-September 1914 Baden-Powell had been enlisted into a job which he described as 'practically Adjutant-General' of the Army. This took him away from the Scouts and, more particularly, the Guides at a time when his presence was badly needed. Olave went into the office one day when Miss Macdonald was unwell and gave considerable clerical assistance for a few days. It must have been pointed out to her that she had no authority for this as Baden-Powell sent a letter to Mrs Lumley Holland explaining the circumstances and suggesting that there should be a second member of staff. Olave also wrote to offer her services to the Committee and Baden-Powell wrote again to suggest that she should represent him on the Committee as he was so engaged with his war duties. At the same time Agnes wrote to the committee to suggest that Olave should be invited to sit on it. The Committee discussed the matter and the members were quite clear that they did not want Olave's help on the Committee and, as she was not a member of the Committee, they considered it inappropriate for her to help in the office. Mrs Lumley Holland then wrote Olave a letter in which she firmly turned down her offer on the grounds that there were already enough Baden-Powells involved in their work. Or was it, perhaps, that Baden-Powell had again taken up the reins of 'their' territory? Sadly, Olave believed throughout her life that the decision not to include her on the Committee had been made by Agnes.

Through the autumn of 1914 Henrietta had a series of slight strokes. On 13 October she died, aged ninety, the causes being given on the death certificate as chronic intestinal obstruction and senile decay. The senile decay must have been of very recent onset for, until shortly before then, she had carried on a vigorous correspondence whenever Agnes was away. Henrietta was buried on 16 October in the family grave at Kensal Green. Her death was a great loss to the family. In the *Girl Guides' Gazette* of 22 October 1914 Baden-Powell wrote a delightful obituary which was obviously intended also as an inspirational piece for the girls. The following month Agnes wrote a similar piece, acknowledging the many expressions of sympathy she had received.

The death of Henrietta removed Agnes' strongest supporter. She had never lived a life independent of the mother who had been her staunchest encourager and supporter. Moreover, most of the family income died with Henrietta whose clever manipulation of money had been unable to make provision for the future. The two family members who most had Agnes' welfare at heart, Stephe and Baden, were caught up with war duties and had little time to spare to help sort out domestic matters. In addition Florence, the wife of Agnes' artist brother, died a few days after Henrietta, so adding to the family's burden of bereavement and disturbance. For the first time in her life Agnes was without anybody to defend her. She went and lived with Frank until he died; however, they had never been close and sadly this was not a happy period. After Frank's death in 1931 Agnes spent much of her time with Baden at his pleasant home at Riverhead, near Sevenoaks in Kent. It was after his death in 1937 that she became rather nomadic.

The Storm Breaks

In November 1914 Miss Macdonald broke ranks and wrote to Olave with a two-fold message for Baden-Powell. The main purport of the letter concerned the relationship between the YWCA and the Girl Guides. The YWCA had been represented on the Committee, in the form of Miss Dashwood, since the early days as the organisation was a keen sponsor of Guide Companies. By the end of 1914 the Guiding organisation within the YWCA was more efficient, and was flourishing better, than the original body. By the time that Miss Macdonald wrote her letter she was seriously concerned that the YWCA was attempting to take over the running of the entire Movement. She added that it was Miss Dashwood who had so strongly opposed Olave's appointment to the Committee.

Miss Macdonald's other, but related, issue concerned Agnes' recent change of status as President. She reported a rumour that Baden-Powell was telling people that it was at his insistence that this had happened; people were saying that, Agnes having done all the spade work, others were now going to reap the kudos. It is quite obvious that Miss Macdonald had a serious fear that there was about to be a split in the Girl Guides.

In fact, Baden-Powell was already aware of problems, having been alerted earlier by Mrs Benson, and he was already making his plans for the Guides to be run under a Charter. Many of the entries in his diary at this time refer to engagements with the Guides and to the pursuance of the Charter. He wrote to Mrs Lumley Holland, the Committee Chairman, a letter that amounted almost to a royal command for a meeting of the Committee to be called as a matter of urgency. He wrote,

> It is a very long time since we have had one, even for routine business. There seem to be no fixed dates of intervals at which Committees are held and it is difficult for my business to be carried on without some regulation in this direction.

He went on to say,

> Where I have asked Company officers their ideas regarding Headquarters, they seem to look entirely to my sister for instruction and information, although she exercises no executive function. They do not know the Headquarters Committee – it seems to be out of touch with them.

The letter goes on to speak of the importance of all pulling together.

When Baden-Powell visited Mrs Lumley Holland to discuss with her the possible resignation of the present members of the Committee she threatened to make public certain allegations against Agnes relating to financial irregularities. It would seem that this related to the continuing misunderstanding relating to the financing of Agnes in the work she was doing for the Girl Guides. Nevertheless it must have shaken Baden-Powell's confidence in his sister's authority. In his diary Baden-Powell wrote of the meeting,

> Called on Mrs. Lumley Holland who, in effect, threatened that if I ejected part of the Girl Guide committee some of them might turn

nasty and expose what she hinted was dishonesty on Az's part in keeping £100 sent to her by Miss Dupre for the Girl Guides and of forwarding £10 to the fund. She said she had something far worse about Az in black and white but would not say what. Confessed she had not heard Az's version of £100. Asked Az. She said Miss Dupre said in enclosing the cheque that it was for her to use as she thought best for the Girl Guides. The [illegible] of expense of pictures in the Gazette had risen so she sent £10 for that to the office, and intended to distribute some more in prizes and paying the [illegible]

It will be recalled that, on an earlier occasion, she had written to her mother of having purchased a gift for presentation to a Guider.

The meeting Baden-Powell had called happened within days and was followed by a succession of further meetings to discuss the Charter. At the insistence of the Committee most of the meetings were also attended by Agnes. It would seem quite clear from the Minutes that Baden-Powell was determined that his sister would continue as President and, equally, that he had a fair idea who would not be on the new Council. By the beginning of 1915 the Charter had been passed by the solicitor and was on the table and ready for signing. There was no doubt who was in charge: Agnes would continue as President, although in her new, non-executive function; Baden-Powell would be the Chairman; the new, enlarged Committee would be drawn from men and women who were experienced in education and training. Clearly the Executive Committee, as Guiding had known it, was out. Towards the end of January Miss Dashwood wrote to Baden-Powell, pressing that Mrs Lumley Holland, at least, should be on the new Council and giving a scarcely veiled implication that Baden-Powell was 'packing' the new Council with his supporters and that the Guides was in danger of becoming 'a one-man show'. Possibly to ease the tension, Olave wrote a letter in June 1915 to The Council of the Girl Guides Association which ran,

> As my name has been suggested for one or other of the Departments in the new Executive of the Girl Guides, I write to ask that I may be excused from serving, as I feel that, with the assistance of my sister-in-law and my husband, already at the head of affairs, it would be becoming too much of a family concern were I also to be associated with it.

At the same time I would not have it understood that I am in any way wanting in interest towards the movement, for on the contrary I am very anxious indeed to do anything I possibly can to help it behind the scenes, for I am convinced of the great possibilities that lie before it; and anything that I can possibly do to help will be done.

The following month Agnes stayed with Baden-Powell and Olave at Ewhurst.

The Girl Guides was established and growing, it was making a great contribution to the war effort, Baden-Powell was at the helm and things at Headquarters seemed to have calmed down. People were able to turn their attention to other things. There was a growing demand among the Guiders for some kind of formal training. And so the GOATS (Girl Guides' Officers' Training School) came into being. It was run by Mrs Agatha Blyth and the approach was completely experiential which, after they had recovered from the initial shock, most of the Guiders thoroughly enjoyed. It set the tone for Guiders' training. When Baden-Powell visited, Mrs Blyth considered that he had been impressed.

Also, towards the end of 1915, Olave made her Guide Promise, thereby becoming eligible to hold office in the Girl Guides. The following February she headed up the Girl Guide Hut Fund Committee, formed to raise funds for the provision of a recreation hut behind the lines in France. Such was the success of her leadership of the project that it was able to provide, not only the hut, but also substantial additions, as well as an ambulance.

It was shortly after the formation of this committee that Baden-Powell noted in his diary that Miss Dashwood had held a small, 'informal', conference of the Girl Guide Committee.

Percy Everett, the Scouting enthusiast who was involved with Pearson's, the company which had published *The Golden Rule*, had not lost interest in the Guides. In the spring of 1916 he was discussing with Baden-Powell the possibility of publishing a weekly paper for the girls. Baden-Powell wrote to him,

My wife and I would be glad to accept it were it not that we are a little afraid of hurting my sister's feelings by seeming to oust her from her position in the Movement. Do you think it would be possible therefore to include her name with ours in the agreement?

It was also at this time that Agnes was compiling a book of eight one-act plays suitable for Girl Guides. While on the lookout for appropriate material she also had to be diplomatic about submissions which she considered unsuitable. She wrote to one contributor, who had first contacted her six months before, 'I find it just a little long for our platforms, otherwise scenes and dress are very suitable.' To give additional weight she signs the letter 'Agnes Baden-Powell, Chief Guide'.

A few months later, at Baden-Powell's suggestion, Olave was appointed Guide County Commissioner for Sussex. She took the county by storm and, within a very short time, had appointed a complete network of Commissioners and Secretaries, something which made a great impact way beyond Sussex. Thus, it was not surprising that, when she attended the first County Commissioners' Conference that October, there was a clamour for her to be appointed Chief Commissioner for the country.

Before the conference Baden-Powell had telephoned Agnes and persuaded her not to attend. This was followed by a letter. However, Olave wrote to ask her view on the proposal which had been made; she wrote, '. . . before saying whether I would accept the position or not I want you to tell me straightly whether you consider that I should be diminishing your authority in any way by so doing.' Agnes told her straightly when she replied, 'I have got your note and write a line to say go at it by all means, no one better fitted for the post.' Thus it was that, at the meeting of the Committee a few days later, Mrs Lumley Holland, no less, proposed Olave's appointment as Chief Commissioner and a member of the Executive Committee. Miss Dashwood was not present. Agnes had given way with her customary, gentle generosity and the lady who had started the Girl Guides was now, completely, a figurehead President.

The following month the Annual Meeting of the Council was held when Olave's election to the Committee was ratified. Immediately afterwards a vote of thanks was proposed by Baden-Powell to the two retiring members, Mrs Lumley Holland and Miss Dashwood. Miss

Dashwood then made an attempt to get the Council to approve the Agreement which had been made between the Committee and the YWCA prior to the introduction of the Charter. The matter was referred to the new Executive Committee. The Girl Guides had entered a new phase without the two women who had dominated its Committee for several years. When Mrs Lumley Holland died in 1929 the Girl Guide badge was inscribed on the foot of her memorial plaque in the family church in Kent.

Olave took up her new appointment with enthusiasm, offering the girls a new, younger appearance to their activities and, within three months, the number of Guides had trebled. She gradually took on the control of more aspects of the Guides, including the Officers' Training School. Baden-Powell had inspected the GOATS and commended it warmly, especially admiring the spirit of the organisation; however, six months later he closed it because he considered that the spirit was out of keeping with that of the Movement. After his second visit, on 10 March 1916, he had written in his diary,

> visit Mrs. Blyth's OTC for Girl Guides. Explained teaching required is not so much for officers to pass badge tests as to know the psychology of the child and inner meaning of the Guide training.

Olave then started a new training organisation.

How Girls Can Help to Build Up the Empire had been the handbook of the Girl Guides for six years. Olave did not like it and referred to it as the 'little blue muddly'. Moreover, Britain was at war and girls were learning new ways. For four years the Guides had been serving the war effort magnificently and, around them, women were doing jobs previously done by men. A more up-to-date publication was needed. As early as March 1916 Baden-Powell had discussed with Agnes the need to update the book and some of the tests. Throughout 1917 Baden-Powell was working on the new book in consultation with Agnes. It should also have been in consultation with a committee but its members do not seem to have been very assiduous in attending meetings. It was about this time that Baden-Powell noted in his diary that Miss Dashwood had held that small 'informal' conference of the Girl Guide committee. Early in 1918, Baden-Powell published his handbook for Guiders, *Girl Guiding*. It seemed to some that it was almost as if there was an attempt to obliterate all evidence of Agnes' hard work in starting the Movement. Indeed, when there was a reception for the Girl Guides at Buckingham Palace, Agnes was not invited. As she was still President she had every right to be there and she went to the reception regardless but was denied admittance. For someone who figured regularly in the *Court Circular* this must have been doubly humiliating. However, she was one of those who greeted Queen Alexandra to a rally of the Girl Guides in Hyde Park in the July of that year. We read in the *Court Circular* that when the Queen, accompanied by Princess Victoria, arrived at the Rally she was greeted by Baden-Powell and Agnes. Olave and Mrs Mark Kerr, a friend of Agnes who was Commissioner for London, were in charge of the Rally and were presented to the Queen later.

A month later Olave progressed, by popular acclaim, from being Chief Commissioner to being Chief Guide.

Just before the Armistice the family home at Princes Gate was sold, the proceeds being divided equally between Henrietta's children.

Over the following eighteen months Agnes had to endure sitting through various Council meetings during which her remaining status was stripped from her. The Annual Report for 1919 reported her resignation from the role of President, giving a pleasant tribute to the work she had done. The resignation was also reported of the Headquarters' secretary, Miss Macdonald, who felt very strongly about the way in which Agnes had been treated. Like Agnes, she had been instrumental in the formation of the Girl Guides and had served the Movement with dedication for ten years.

At an extraordinary meeting of the Council held in February 1920, a resolution was passed whereby the President would be elected annually at the Annual General Meeting and would be a non-executive role. This meeting was obviously held to precede the AGM at which the annual report announcing Agnes' resignation would be presented.

Agnes' last appearance on the national scene was at the London Guide Rally when it was announced that Princess Mary had accepted the position of President and that, in future, Agnes would be a Vice-President. In a photograph of the occasion Mrs Kerr and Percy Everett, who are looking determinedly cheerful, are accompanying Princess

Mary who is looking worried or bewildered and Agnes, looking defeated, is several paces behind. To all intents and purposes her role in Guiding had ended.

PART III

Once a Guide

ONCE A GUIDE

Agnes was deeply hurt by the way she had been treated. Fortunately she had a number of good friends, including Professor and Mrs Burkett of Cambridge, who gave her great support at this time and helped her to come to terms with what had happened.

However, there is a well-known saying, 'Once a Guide, always a Guide'. In the case of Agnes this was certainly true. She had started the Movement and she intended to finish as one of its members. The hierarchy may have decided to dispense of her services but the Movement at large was proud of her as she was of it, and continued to want her. For the rest of her life Agnes would refer to herself as 'the Grandmother of the Girl Guides'.

Guiding In Essex . . .

Agnes was still in uniform. In 1917 she had been appointed County Commissioner for Essex and that appointment continued.

Essex is a large county, which has since been divided for Guiding purposes into three, and at that time it had large divisions. Each division followed the boundary of a Parliamentary constituency which meant, for instance, that the Maldon Division stretched for forty miles across. Even with today's transport, such a size would be deemed unmanageable. At that early stage there was still a lot to be done in organising the county, and it cannot have been easy to do it from Wimbledon, where Agnes was living at that time.

Among the appointments she made was that of a County Camp Advisor to whom Agnes sent a postcard of welcome on which she had painted a beautiful, many coloured parrot. She addresses her as 'My dear Advisor' and the card is couched in such welcoming terms as to make one prepared to go crawling on one's knees to do her bidding.

County meetings for the commissioners were held at the Liverpool Street Hotel. This would have made sense as it was accessible to all those attending. One person, present at a meeting in 1923, noted that,

> all Commissioners were not correctly dressed – at least one had her hat on back to front and hatpins were visible . . . At this meeting several very forceful ladies were not as polite as they might have been to the Chairman who was not very businesslike.

The same writer goes on to say,

> Miss Baden-Powell wore a hat not turned up at the side and trimmed with a gold cord round it. She was a very gentle and charming lady, but not very practical.

What is not mentioned is that, at that time, Agnes was wearing a Guide badge made of real gold. She says in a letter of 1917 that it was 'presented to me by the Girl Guides at the Gold mine in Australia'. Agnes was quite capable of going there but it seems unlikely that she did, since no record exists of what would have been an expensive visit. Or was it perhaps given to her brother to be passed on to her? Or the Australian Guides may have visited England.

In 1922 there was a world-wide conference for Guide commissioners held at Newnham College, Cambridge. Agnes attended this in her capacity as County Commissioner for Essex. What she was not supposed to attend was a World Camp which was held at Foxlease in the summer of 1924. Agnes had, in fact, been forbidden to go but nevertheless she did, although she had to spend much of her time dodging out of sight of those who might wish to eject her. Many of the people there were contacts that she had made, and who she counted among her friends, and it was only to be expected that she should wish to see them, not to mention that she had a lively interest in the camp and its activities.

In 1924 it was decided that 'Essex needed stricter handling' and that a new County Commissioner should be appointed. Agnes was, by then, past sixty-five, the age at which Guiders are now expected to cease uniformed Guiding. However, she still did not feel ready to stop. A minute of the national Executive Committee in January 1925 reads,

The Chief Commissioner reported that in view of the need of a change in the County Commissionership of Essex as expressed by the Commissioners of the County, it had become necessary to appoint a new County Commissioner.

It was agreed that a letter be written to Miss Baden-Powell, telling her that another County Commissioner had been appointed for Essex, and asking her to become County President for Essex as from February 1st 1925.

In the following month's minutes it is reported that Agnes had resigned and that her successor had been appointed. The successor lived in Essex, which was counted to be an advantage. It is reported that, on occasions, the new County Commissioner wore over her uniform a cloak rather like that of a policeman.

Agnes' last remembered official appearance in Essex was some time later, when she attended the opening of the large Greater London Camping Site at Grange Farm in Chigwell.

. . . AND BEYOND

The Girl Guide Movement was Agnes' baby, and it is a rare mother who can abandon her child. Agnes never ceased to take an interest in Guides, wherever she came across them, and she would look in on any camp or training session which she happened to be near. She still wore a uniform when she considered that the occasion warranted it, albeit a uniform of her own design. And why not? After all it was she who had designed the first uniform. It is reckoned that, until she was in her eighties, she was still spending about three months in each year under canvas and she retained a vital interest in all those things which go to make up the grand game of Guiding. About ten years ago a number of people put down on paper their recollections of meeting Agnes and, in the next few pages, they will speak for themselves:

Peggy Johnson of Victoria wrote:

One summer in the early nineteen-twenties I, a Guide in a school company in St. Marylebone, took part with my sister, a Guide in another school company in St. Marylebone, in an indoor training weekend at Hornchurch in Essex. Among the august VIPs was Miss Agnes Baden-Powell. I was a member of the patrol that was allotted cooks' duties on the first morning. I remember very well Miss Baden-Powell coming into the kitchen at an early hour and requesting a cup of tea. To my embarrassment, not to say shame, I had never made tea before, and ever since then I have thought that my product must have been the worst cup of tea she ever tasted, for I am sure that I never let the water boil, and the tea-leaves must have been floating around in the cup! However, tactfully, the dear lady made no comment!

Another letter came from Eileen Nobbs of Norfolk. Her memory went:

Whilst living at Lowestoft in my young days, I was a very active and keen Guide and worked hard for badges and my 'Gold Cords'. I was rewarded by being invited to attend a service at Westminster Abbey for Scouts and Guides. Three of us girls together with our Lieutenant duly went to London by car. This would be about 1932-3 but I cannot recall why this service took place. We had seats in the choir stalls of the Abbey and it was a magic moment seeing Lord Baden-Powell walk past us towards the altar.

Now, our Guide Captain, quite an elderly lady, knew Miss Agnes and she arranged for us to meet her for tea at a nearby cafe after the service. I think we were all a bit nervous of meeting such a personality but she soon put us at ease as we chatted together. We felt it was a momentous occasion. She was quite a charming softly spoken lady and we were sorry to leave her presence.

Betty Vokins of Enfield wrote to say that she met Agnes in 1934/5:

I was a Guide in the 2nd Palmers Green Company. We were camping at Nutley, Sussex, on a private estate owned by Lord Castle Stewart in the Ashdown Forest area. We had no reason to be honoured by such a visit . . .

After explaining the disappointment when none of her photographs came out, Betty ended:

> To my young eyes she appeared an old lady – she was wearing uniform.

Constance Ife (née Grace) of Lewes recalled meeting Agnes in 1936 at a function in London and kept her autograph as a treasured possession.

One correspondent who took the trouble to write out her story in full was Margaret Pettigrew (née Moir) of Edinburgh:

> <u>The Day I served Lunch to Agnes Baden-Powell</u>
>
> It happened in July 1937 at the Scottish International Camp held at Blair Atholl Castle grounds, Perthshire, Scotland. During the middle weekend Agnes Baden-Powell camped with us in a ridge tent, right in the centre of the sub-camps and not far from the flag pole. For each meal she visited the sub-camps in turn. She was a lovely lady. Our turn came for a lunch meal and, as I was on Quartermaster duty, I had the privilege of serving Agnes Baden-Powell. (I felt like offering it on my knees.)
>
> On the Saturday evening she joined us for camp fire, sitting on her camp chair. On the Sunday, as each camp marched off to church, we passed Agnes Baden-Powell sitting on her chair just outside her tent. She acknowledged us all. We felt as though we were on a Grand March, passing a saluting base.

Margaret was sixteen years old at the time and said what an honour she had considered it to be one of the six Guides chosen to represent the City of Glasgow at the Camp.

Sister Mary Stella CSP of Surrey wrote, with a story which reminds us of Agnes' life-long involvement in the Red Cross, of an incident which happened at the end of the summer term of 1937/8:

> I was the leader of our school Red Cross Cadet team who won the Lady Northcote Trophy in that year. We were bidden to the Duke of York's Headquarters for the presentation of the trophy, at a general presentation of medals and such. It was quite an occasion. As I stepped

down from the dais with the trophy, an elderly lady stepped forward to congratulate me, and looked at my various badges. "I might have known", she said, "that it would be a Guide to win a thing like this." I just smiled sweetly, not knowing who she was, and she went on, "I was a Girl Guide too, the very first one." At which point another award was called and she melted back into the crowd, and I didn't see her again. I asked our Commandant if she knew who the lady was and she told me that she was Agnes Baden-Powell.

A correspondent whose encounter with Agnes resulted in a further meeting and who later presented the relevant correspondence to the Guide Archives is Vivienne Constantinides of Surrey:

In 1939 the 1st Kenwood and 5th West Finchley Guide Companies held a joint camp in the beautiful grounds of Oldlands Hall, the lovely home of Sir Bernard and Miss Hermionie Eckstein (Division Commissioner for North Middlesex from 1932 to 1945.) Miss Agnes was one of the many weekend guests there and came down to our field with them to join in our camp fire sing-song one evening. In fact she actually spent a night 'under canvas' with us! I have a recollection of her in immaculate Guide uniform on a bright dewy morning, standing outside her tent waiting to be summoned to morning prayers and breakfast!

I had taken photographs of the occasion which I promised to send her. This resulted in an exchange of most interesting letters and an invitation to take tea with her at the HQ of the British Red Cross when she was in London.

In the same Division was a Guider, Valerie Garlick, who wrote that Hermionie Eckstein was Division Commissioner and

she took a home during the war at Luton also taking Agnes Baden-Powell to live there, who organised Treasure Hunts in the garden when we camped there . . . I also remember she came to one of our enrolments in Whetstone.

Sylvia Smith of Salisbury wrote:

My meeting with Agnes Baden-Powell was on Saturday 14th August 1943. At the time I was a very young Guide enjoying my first camp at Kimpton. It being wartime we had actually pitched our camp under trees on, I believe, land belonging to the then County Commissioner for Hertfordshire. On that day I recall our thrill at hearing that we were to have a very distinguished visitor to our campfire. I can remember her coming and joining us at that event, her only concession to her age being that she sat on a little three-legged stool instead of sitting on the ground like the rest of us.

A final offering came from Margaret Smith of Golders Green:

Many years ago when I was a young Guider on my way to a training camp with some friends, at the ticket barrier of a main line station, a strange little old lady seemed excited to see us. She asked the usual questions and frequently said, 'I'm a little Brownie' which became a catchphrase among us, I'm sorry to say. I can't remember which station, probably Victoria or Waterloo, or where the camp was held, but it must have been very near her home for the next day she turned up to 'inspect the camp' and to speak to us, wearing her version of a Guider's uniform.

Agnes Baden-Powell was a remarkable woman who must not be forgotten and deserves recognition with her brother. I was thrilled to own a copy of 'How Girls Can Help to Build the Empire', and wondered about her then, for it contained so much skill and knowledge of so much.

Now that I am very old I am proud that I remember meeting Agnes Baden-Powell.

Agnes' contact with the Guides in Cambridge remained strong. In 1941, on Sunday 15 June, she was an honoured guest, along with her longstanding friend Marguerite de Beaumont, at the dedication in St Peter's Church of the 1st Barton Guides' World Flag. The flag is quite tattered now but it retains an honoured place, along with the invitation to the service signed by the principal guests, in the archives of the Company.

A FIRST CLASS GUIDE

The purpose of the great game of Guiding is to equip girls to play a constructive part in the life of the world. To this end they are encouraged to develop skills in every possible direction: in the arts, in woodcraft, in medicine, in sport, in homecraft and, of course, in the development of their spiritual and emotional selves. By the time she started the Girl Guides Agnes Baden-Powell had long been a fully equipped First Class Girl Guide. We know of the many organisations in which she was involved, although sadly they do not all have good archives and some organisations, which have ceased to exist, are untraceable.

Air Travel

Stephe, Agnes and Baden, as a little group at the end of the large Baden-Powell family, were always close together. If anything, Agnes appears to have been closest to Baden. This may have been because Baden was the youngest but it is more likely to have been because Stephe, the future General and founder of Scouting, tended by nature to be rather more of a loner. What is certain is that Agnes and Baden shared many interests. This was seen particularly in their shared love of flying which was the great passion of Baden's life.

Initially their interest was in ballooning. Balloon ascents were popular spectacles throughout the nineteenth century and, by the time they were in their twenties, Baden and Agnes were thoroughly involved. This was not a cheap pastime and they had to find ways of doing it as economically as possible. Agnes would help Baden to make the balloons by obtaining the silk and using her excellent needlework skills to work it into the envelopes. Once the balloons were made she would share with him in his flights, including those from Crystal Palace, and the couple became well known in ballooning circles. Baden, like his older brother, was making his career in the Army where he pursued his ballooning, becoming an expert on the use of balloons and kites for military purposes.

By the end of the century the aeroplane was beginning to be significant. This, of course, was merely an extension of the balloon and

Baden and Agnes embraced it with enthusiasm. It is hardly surprising that with the arrival of the aeroplane Baden, in particular, and Agnes were right in the vanguard of those ready to experiment with the new form of air transport. There can be little doubt that, had they been wealthier, both would have done many hours as pilots. As it was, although Agnes flew a great deal with Baden (usually from Hendon), she never actually gained her pilot's licence.

In 1897 Baden founded *The Aeronautical Journal*, the technical journal of The Aeronautical Society (later to receive royal patronage) and went on to become the Honorary Secretary of the Society and, in due course, its first President.

In 1903 Baden would retire from the Army, much to the disgust of his mother, in order to found the scientific journal *Knowledge* which, sadly, foundered after a short life. This left him with additional time to devote to the Royal Aeronautical Society.

Agnes, herself, made a significant impact on the Royal Aeronautical Society. In 1938, following Baden's death from heart trouble in the previous year, Agnes created the Baden-Powell Memorial Prize, to be presented twice yearly to the best candidate in the Associate Fellowship Examinations of the Society. On some occasions this proved of inestimable value in enabling research to be carried out that would otherwise have been impossible. Following this, the Council agreed unanimously that she should be made an Honorary Companion of the Society. She was only the second woman to be so honoured. In recognition of her Honorary Companionship Agnes was presented with a diamond encrusted replica of the Society's badge, a flying kestrel.

As was shown earlier Agnes was adept at cycling, hunting, fishing and possibly fencing. It is hardly surprising that the only surviving sister in a family of boys should have a well developed interest in all forms of sport.

Agnes' other skills matured with the years. Queen Mary's Clothing Guild was a natural outlet for her, combining as it did needlework and charitable work. Its purpose was to provide clothes for needy people, and during the First World War it supplied comforts for troops at the front. Between the wars the Guild was supplying an average of 60,000 garments a year.

The League of Mercy was an organisation which not only enjoyed Agnes' patronage but of which she was the local President. The Foundation was invaluable in the days before the National Health Service; its members assisted with the maintenance and work of the many voluntary hospitals and the Foundation would seem to be a precursor of today's Leagues of Friends.

Another organisation to enjoy Agnes' patronage was the Royal Empire Society, which subsequently became the Royal Commonwealth Society. All of the Baden-Powells were interested in the Empire, as it was then known. A friend of Baden-Powell's, on a visit to England, had said what a wonderful settler Agnes would make and had tried to persuade her to go to one of the colonies.

A rather stern sounding organisation was the Duty and Discipline Movement. Again the influence for Agnes' involvement appears to be her brother's – Baden-Powell was a member and had written for them leaflet number thirty-two in a series of forty entitled 'British Discipline'. The Movement had its offices in close proximity to those of the Scouts in Queen Victoria Street. It had two objectives: 'to combat softness, slackness, indifference and indiscipline' and 'to give reasonable support to all legitimate authority'.

The Red Cross Society was formed when Agnes was in her early twenties and its humanitarian objectives would have appealed strongly to the idealism that was in her. Therefore it is not surprising that she should have joined it soon after it was established in Britain. By the Second World War she was a Vice-President of the Westminster Division and she held that position until her death.

Agnes was deeply involved and she received the British Red Cross War Medal, awarded to those whose unpaid service amounted to not less than 1,000 hours, for her work in the First World War. The Westminster Division had the largest number of hospitals, four in total, and included the greatest number of beds in the County of London Branch. It also opened hostels for refugees and for VAD workers. The work in the Division also included air-raid work responding to thirty-six calls, working parties, one of which made 22,786 articles, and running thirty-six training classes covering the subjects of First Aid (sixteen), Home Nursing (sixteen) Hygiene (three) and one mysteriously labelled as 'Miscellaneous'. In addition, the Division raised £1, 888 11s through its collecting boxes, the largest sum in the Branch by nearly £500. It is of little surprise to learn that the very active working party continued after the War.

So far as young people were concerned it was reported in 1914 that a Red Cross officer had charge of the Scout orderlies in the borough of Battersea and had organised a 'calling up' system which worked admirably, with the Scouts and Guides rendering splendid assistance.

There were innovations after the War. In 1922 the Westminster Division took over the management of the thirty-two children in the Olga Lyn Day Nursery. It was in the same year that the County of London Red Cross proposed holding a Branch camp. This idea, however, was abandoned as only one Division could definitely guarantee that ten of its members would be present. Could one, perhaps, hazard a guess that the Division which could give the guarantee was the one in which the idea had originated?

The Red Cross in London at this time was much involved in teaching both the Guides and the Scouts, with several Divisions, including Westminster, making a special feature of it. A report at the time stated,

In Kensington a Red Cross officer has been appointed representative on the London Girl Guides Association since 1919, and the Division has done a considerable amount of examining in ambulance and sick nursing. The examinations have been standardised and a Board of Examiners appointed. All examiners must hold recognised First Aid and Home Nursing certificates, and satisfy the Board that they are qualified to examine. Nearly 400 candidates have been examined during the year, and ten Girl Guide companies have received coaching. There is much room for development of this work and the training of the juvenile organisations might become a very important part of the work of Voluntary Aid Detachments.

In 1923 it was reported that,

One new [Red Cross] Junior Unit has been raised in the Marylebone Division and it is satisfactory to record that the training and examining of Boy Scouts and Girl Guides in First Aid and Home Nursing by Officers and members of Voluntary Aid Detachments is extending. There is still a wide field of usefulness in this direction.

In 1924 Red Cross work with Scouts, Guides and other junior organisations was reported as continuing to grow. In 1928 in the Westminster Division, it was reported that the entire establishment was female. The following year the Red Cross manned the First Aid post at the camp which the Scouts held at Earls Court. In 1933 the Agnes Baden-Powell Trophy was presented for competition work in the Westminster Division.

For the rest of her life Agnes would be involved in the work of the Westminster Red Cross, work that included such things as helping in hospitals and specialist clinics and, for the junior members, helping in nurseries and binding library books for hospitals.

KEEPING UP APPEARANCES

By the 1930s Agnes was approaching her eighties. For many women of her time this would have meant, if not already there, sliding gently into old age, but not for Agnes who remained indefatigable. One friendship at that time, which obviously gave great mutual pleasure, was with the Secretary of the Royal Aeronautical Society, Captain Pritchard, with whom she carried on a spasmodic but friendly correspondence. As she approached her eightieth birthday a columnist in *Pearson's Weekly* noted that she still held executive positions in eight organisations, and went on to say that she regarded hard work, good sleep and a sound digestion as the recipe for a long, active and useful life.

Her social life went on unabated and she continued to appear from time to time in the *Court Circular*. In March 1935 it was noted there that Agnes had held the fifth of a series of receptions at the Hans Crescent Hotel where the many distinguished guests who had accepted invitations included the Ambassadors and their wives from Japan, Spain, Argentina, Italy, Switzerland, China, Latvia, Lithuania and Estonia.

In March 1938 Agnes was 'commanded by their majesties' to attend a function at Buckingham Palace. Then, as she approached her eightieth birthday in December that year, there was a long article, entitled 'Agnes Baden-Powell and her Recollections', in the *Council Fire*, the journal of the World Association of Girl Guides and Girl Scouts. The accompanying picture shows Agnes in the uniform of her own design: a (presumably navy) belted suit and broad brimmed hat, with light coloured shirt and tie; on one side there is her Guide badge and all round cords and, on the other, her Red Cross badges. However, an indication of the extent to which she has faded into the background is given in the way in which the article, after saying that she looks twenty years younger than her age, concentrates entirely on the past and says nothing about Agnes' present activities.

A better birthday tribute was paid to her by the *Sunday Dispatch* which, on a page with an article about the Chief Scout, printed a photograph of Agnes touching her toes and, under the title 'And His Sister Still Enjoys Life, Too' wrote,

So that she can cut her birthday cake 'above the clouds', Miss Agnes Baden-Powell is to celebrate her 80th birthday on December 16 with a balloon ascent.

She has also arranged a 10-mile horseback ride, a long swim in an open-air pool, and a night under canvas on a palliasse. If the pool is frozen over, then Miss B-P will write her age with her skates on the ice.

Originally this 5 ft-and-a-bit sister of the Chief Scout planned to ride from London to Nottingham in her balloon, "but friends thought it might be a little too much for me," she told the 'Sunday Dispatch', "so I shall only ride the last ten miles . . . I shall take my birthday cake up in the balloon so I can cut it above the clouds." She added, "I wanted to light the candles up there too, but the pilot said 80 candles alight would be dangerous."

And how has this compact, sturdy little body kept so supple for nearly 80 years? "Plenty of exercise, though I've not bothered much with regular physical jerks. But I can still swing my legs over my head and tap the floor with my feet."

Unhampered by her long tweed coat and hat, down on the floor Miss B-P went. And hoopla! over her head went her strong little legs, and rat-a-tat went her feet on the floor. *A dozen times she did it, like a clockwork toy up and down among the Victorian knick-knacks of her London rooms*. Then we had touching toes, squatting tailor fashion on the floor, and trunk rotation. "But I don't do exercises nearly regularly enough."

A more conventional eightieth birthday party and one at which it was presumably possible to entertain more visitors, was held at the Ladies' Carlton Club.

The outbreak of the Second World War saw Agnes on her metal. She laid siege to the War Office to persuade them to allow women to play a full part, offering to teach a group of women to use a rifle so that they could join the Local Defence Volunteers (the Home Guard). A newspaper article described this octogenarian's recreations as including swimming and dancing. There was little indication anywhere that, like most of her family, she suffered from heart trouble. On one occasion she had stayed with Stephe and Olave for recuperation. There is an undated note from her, probably written on a later occasion, which reads,

> My dear sister Guide,
> I was so pleased to get your note and was much touched by your very kind sympathy. The doctor insists on my lying flat as my heart is so strained. Shall be well very soon.

In April the following year Agnes had been on a Red Cross tour of inspection. But it was not all work: in a letter to her in the same month Captain Pritchard wrote, 'I expect you will be camping for Whitsun . . .'

Life got somewhat tougher for Agnes later in the year. As a result of her home being hit by a bomb she became somewhat nomadic and her health became less good. In a letter to Captain Pritchard in February 1941 she wrote from the Norfolk Hotel in Harrington Road, 'I have been ill ever since Christmas, and am now conquering pneumonia and a touch of pleurisy. Owing to this and my home being bombed . . .'

By the time of her birthday that year Agnes had moved to No.3 Redcliffe Street in Fulham. Guests at her birthday party included Lord Ebishun, Sir Percy Everitt, Lord Plunder, R. B. Bennett and Lord Semphill. By then it had become Captain Pritchard's custom to write a poem for Agnes in celebration of each birthday about which one critic said, 'The verses have a musical ring and quite a flavour of the Seventeenth Century.'

It was not long before Agnes, like most people at that time, was coping with a notable increase in war work. Later in the year she sent to the Royal Aeronautical Society a memorial medal of the Air Ship Z4 which had been cast from its remains. With it she enclosed 'To a Poet' which had been written by a Girl Guide, Margaret Tennyson, for the Girl Guides' Christmas card that year.

In March 1942 Agnes had one of her bright ideas. She wrote to Miss Florence Barwood, Captain Pritchard's secretary, acknowledging receipt of an enamelled badge of the Royal Aeronautical Society (had the jewelled one been lost in the bombing? It has been impossible to trace it). She then went on to suggest a uniform for the Society, and enclosed a design. It would be in Air Force blue with silver buttons all down the lapels. Agnes suggested that it would save washing. Underneath Miss Barwood has written, 'Oh yeah'.

Following her birthday that year Agnes wrote to Captain Pritchard, thanking him for his birthday poem and assuring him that it had been read out by Lord Ebishun and shown around to all at one of her <u>five</u> birthday parties. She continued,

> Unworthy as I am of such an honour, you have outdone Browning and Laurence Binyon and Sir Edwin Arnold as they only wrote verses to my birds and my tame butterflies and my bees.

In 1943 Agnes was living at the Woodmere Hotel in Kensington. There are so many reasons why this may have been so: staffing, housing, heating, rations. Initially she was paying her faithful retainer, Jackson, 14/6 a week but this soon ceased. By this time Olave was back in England, following Baden-Powell's death, and she seems to have visited Agnes about once every three weeks. At this time Agnes was keeping a diary in a small account book and it would seem that the degree to which she had pushed herself was at last having its effect. For much of the time she was unwell, being much bothered with colds, coughs, sore throats and rheumatism. Nevertheless, she was keeping her scrap book up-to-date (a Baden-Powell obsession) with cuttings giving news of the War, and displaying a special interest in the Women's Royal Naval Service. Fortunately her health began to improve as spring warmed up. There were many air raids at this time and it would seem probable that this might have contributed towards her poor health. And yet she seemed quite fearless. Following a luncheon given in her honour at the Forum Club in Grosvenor Gardens, when the flying bombs were at their worst, Agnes declined the offer of a lift home saying, 'No thank you; I shall walk.' And she did.

Birthday Poems by Captain J. Laurence Pritchard, Secretary of the Royal Aeronautical Society

1940 – On an Eighty-Second Birthday

As the passing years are reckoned,
One might say the eighty-second
Is getting on in years.
But what are years to one so young,
So bright of eye and quick of tongue,
No passing time she fears.

Happy birthdays come and go
And friends appreciation show
By coming to a party.
And may another eighteen come
To make a century the sum,
And find you hale and hearty!

1941 – On Birthdays

Some people think it quite absurd,
When they have reached their eighty-third
To be considered old.
For what is eighty odd or more
To those who make a century score
Their aim, so I am told?

Some ladies when they're eighty-three
Write to their friends, 'Please come to tea
'I'm going to hold a party.'
Along they come, but children they
In eyes so smiling and so gay,
So lively, hale and hearty.
And there the lady, young, presides
The youngest still of all Girl Guides,
Her praises still unsung.
At eighty-three she's still, it seems,
The little lady of my dreams
The lady always young.

1942 – On an Eighty-Fourth Birthday

Eighty-four! Eighty-four!
One year more! One year more!
The little lady's going strong.
Four score and four's a lengthy span,
Three score and ten's enough for man,
The little lady's life is long.

And may I be with her to see
The coming of her century.
Then will I praise with pen and tongue
A little lady a century young.

1943 – From a Young Man to a Young Lady on Her Birthday

She's eighty-five
And still alive,
Mirabile dictu!
The kind of girl
Sets hearts awhirl,
The kind of girl to stick to!
I like her style,

I like her smile,
I like her little tricks.
And sure, next year
I'll see my dear
When she is eighty-six.

And I don't doubt
She'll be not out
In 1959.
One hundred years
She'll be, my dears,
And still, I hope be mine.

1944 – Agnes Baden-Powell

My dear, you're really eighty-six?
I can't believe you can be that,
For you're so full of all the tricks
I think sometimes you're only six,
I don't believe you, that is flat!

No my dear, you're far too young
To make me think you're getting old
Though every year your praise I've sung.
Years do not matter to the young,
And never will to hearts of gold.

And so, my dear, as Time goes by,
I find you're younger every year.
So may I always live to cry
Your praises and not wonder why
You're ever young my dear.

AGE SHALL NOT WEARY HER

Sadly the century to which Captain Pritchard's poems looked forward was not to happen. It is useless to say 'what if' but, the way things had been for Agnes at the beginning of the War, it seems quite possible to suggest that, had it not been for the stresses which those years imposed, the century might have been quite feasible.

In April 1945 Agnes was staying at a hotel in Kingston, Surrey. On 25 April she had a fall, as a result of which she was admitted two days later to the London Homeopathic Hospital which was in its wartime premises just nearby, Coombe Woodhouse on Coombe Hill, and letters were sent to notify her relatives. On 14 May her niece, Maud Moore, sent a letter to her brother, Donald Baden-Powell, saying that Agnes was going downhill and suggesting that he should visit. On 26 of that month her situation was sufficiently grave for Donald, who, with Maud, was named as an executor, to contact Agnes' solicitor.

Agnes died on 6 June 1945. The Second World War had just ended. Agnes had so been looking forward to the end of the War in anticipation of being able to learn how to fly a helicopter. Rose Kerr wrote in her book, *Here Come the Girl Guides*, 'Without her courage, originality, and untiring labour in the early years the feminine offshoot of the Boy Scouts would never have found its feet and become the great force which it is today.' Percy Everett, in the obituary he wrote for *The Guider* quoted from one of her recent letters,

> I had a lovely time camping out in August, when it was very hot, and I had to test the Guides in measuring the height of trees. Then we had fire-lighting competitions and lots of fun.

The funeral took place, conducted by the Revd B. C. H. Andrews, on Friday, 8 June at Kensal Green Cemetery where Agnes was buried in the family grave. Agnes' death and her funeral were reported widely. Many people were present at the funeral where they were headed by Mrs Schofield (representing Lady Baden-Powell who was unable to be present), Mrs John King (Heather Baden-Powell), Mr and Mrs Harvey Moore (Maud) and Mrs Jackson, Agnes' faithful retainer.

Representatives of her many activities were headed by Baden-Powell's good friend, Percy Everett from the Boy Scouts and Finola, Lady Somers, who was Chief Commissioner of the Girl Guides. Following the funeral a lady called Ada Godson wrote to Maud,

> 'Im so glad Agnes had such a lovely morning – it rained heavily after lunch. The more I think of Agnes . . . the more marvellous she appears to have been. I remember her taking dancing lessons in my studio when she must have been almost eighty and then informing me she would like to join my party at a dance shortly afterwards. An artist phoned me up the other day and asked after her and said he remembered dancing with her on that occasion and she danced so well. I have just come across the plan of the luncheon party we arranged for her eightieth birthday at the Ladies' Carlton. I see we had ninety-five covers – proof of her popularity? . . .'

Agnes' executors were her niece and nephew, Maud and Donald. Her solicitor wrote to Donald, who was still overseas at the time, saying that he had enjoyed her custom for over 45 years. There was, by this time, very little to leave. Many of her possessions had been lost when her flat was bombed. The gross amount raised by the sale of her furniture and effects was £384 5s 6d.

There were many obituaries, not just in Guiding circles but in most of the regional papers. It would seem that a press release had been sent out for there is a great similarity in them, yet many of them included warm personal tributes. Great stress was laid on the fact that she was the founder of the Girl Guides and many of the obituaries referred to her as 'Girl Guide Number One'.

ACROSS THE POND

Until the abolition of the First Class Badge in 1968, a knowledge of Agnes was essential for the history element of the badge. Thereafter she became virtually forgotten until her handbook was reprinted in facsimile in the early 1990s. And then the author heard that she was still remembered in the Ontario Province of Canada where the AGGIE was held annually on the last weekend in April.

The AGGIE, which was an activity weekend for the Senior Section (girls in their later teens), was started in 1973. Agnes had visited Canada in 1931 when she had made a great impression on the local Guide community. Some years later it was written that, 'Guides were amazed at her talents . . . but most of all she enjoyed visiting Guides all over the world.'

Over the years since the start of the weekends AGGIE has had an adventurous life. She has taken part in the Olympics and visited Niagara Falls, she has met the Mounties, seen the Northern Lights, ridden a magic carpet, been on the Southern Belle and done a Highland Fling; she has tiptoed through the tulips, visited King Arthur's Court and even met Romeo, something which would probably have been a great success for the real Agnes. There is a large AGGIE doll which was held for the year by the Area which was hosting the next event and, each year, the doll was dressed in clothes appropriate for the theme of the weekend. There now exists a very large suitcase of AGGIE's wardrobe which travelled with her. Agnes, with her great love of clothes, would greatly have appreciated that.

The weekend, in many ways, included the sort of activities that one would find at a similar event anywhere in the Guiding world. There were quizzes and outings and a campfire and explorations of various issues. Inevitably there was time to drink coffee and put the world to rights. On the Saturday night there was a banquet which was attended by Guide dignitaries; there the major awards of the year are given out. The families of the award winners were also invited to attend this event, but after the dinner.

The year that the author attended the weekend she was invited to talk to the girls about Agnes. Although they had played about with her name for many years they actually knew very little about her and the talk was warmly received.

Sadly, enquiries have elicited the information that the AGGIE event has recently been discontinued, and that is a pity.

Epilogue

Many years ago Cynthia Forbes, who was at that time Assistant Archivist at Guide Headquarters, gave a talk to the Girl Guides Association AGM called 'If it hadn't been for Agnes'. It is, of course, impossible to say what might have happened if Agnes had not responded to her brother's request to start the sister movement to the Scouts. We know that Baden-Powell had already asked at least two other women to do the job before persuading Agnes who, although wonderfully equipped in so many ways for the task, was in other ways quite unsuitable – something he must have known. However, of one thing we can be quite certain, if it hadn't been for Agnes millions of girls throughout the world would quite likely have missed out on an adventure of a lifetime. And it is because Guiding, for so many, has become the adventure of a lifetime, that we have here what some of those women have said about what a lifetime's Guiding has meant to them.

It is not unusual to find several members of a family in Guiding. In Hyde in Cheshire there is such a family, all of whom have offered comments. Great-grandmother, Vera Porter, who is ninety-one says,

> In the Guides I made longstanding friends and it gave me lifelong skills which have been invaluable all through my life.

Grandmother, Dorothea Charlton, who is sixty-seven wrote,

> My friends in the Guides became my best friends, we enjoyed life and everything we did together in the Guides. The discipline and skills of working together with consideration and support for others is something I've never forgotten and have tried to practise all my life.

Her daughter, Nicola Hewitt, who is forty says,

> Being a Guide prepared me for life situations and gave me lots of experiences I would never have had – and – it was the beginning of some lifelong friendships.

And what of the present generation? Great-grand-daughter, Phoebe Hewitt who, at seven, is still at the beginning of her Guiding career, writes,

> I like going to Brownies because I do lots of fun activities with my friends. I liked going to the Centenary Celebrations in Southport and I got enrolled by the Chief Guide! I loved being a Rainbow.

Claire Lunney of Suffolk says,

> Guiding to me embodies all that is ideal for young people. From enrolment as a Brownie in South Wales in 1942 to my subsequent appointment as Suffolk's County Guide President, my involvement with Guiding continues to be an important and immense privilege.

Another person who has come to Suffolk from elsewhere is Pam Cowee who did most of her Guiding in Surrey and Cheshire (Stockport County). She says that Guiding has given her skills for life, international friends – and oodles of fun. Shirley Burwell (formerly S. D. Pethers) writes,

> I would like you to know that I had a wonderful time in Guiding in London and camping in Chigwell Row. I was Guide Captain in St. Martin's East Ham and this meant so very much to me. And the outings with the Brownies and Guides were so good. And then I was Secretary, visiting all the companies. This meant so much to me. Then Trefoil Guild in West Ham, London.

Shirley, too, has now come to live in Suffolk.
Ann Haseler of Cheltenham writes,

Guiding (and Scouting) is a way of life and a lifetime's pleasure. It has given me a multitude of friends, pleasurable responsibilities and above all, my family, as I met my husband through the University Scout and Guide Club.

Muriel Frost, another person from Suffolk, writes,

Guiding for me, as an adult, has meant the satisfaction of working with like-minded people to help run a worthwhile organisation for the girls, the value of the friendships and the mutual support involved, and the feeling of 'belonging', country- as well as county-wide, wherever you may meet 'Guidey' people.

And Ann Mitchell MBE of Cambridge writes,

I am sure Agnes could not have foreseen a world movement of such size and influence. I have been truly blessed to experience World Guiding in so many places, especially Our Chalet, And to have had the chance to run a Guide Company for forty years and be a part of so many young lives.

Returning to Cheshire, Betty Dicks says,

As a child life was very austere. There was no money available for activities I longed to do, such as music, horse riding or holidays. Then as I grew older I discovered 'Guiding' which opened up a new life, a life that included Promise, Faith in God, friendship, singing, camping, outdoor activities, a love of nature and confidence to do things that I never thought I would be able to do. Guiding made me realise that, whatever material things you possess, it's what you are inside that matters, which in turn has an effect on the lives of those around you.

On another occasion Betty had written,

Isn't Guiding wonderful? We only need to spend an hour or so together and we are old friends. Where else would you experience such friendships?

Betty's friend, Marjorie Ashurst, writes,

> I came into the Movement as a young adult, keen, enthusiastic, eager. Guiding gave me a Promise to keep, fun, friendship, and a love of camping, all of which at the age of 75 I am still enjoying.

Irene Ball, from the same Trefoil Guild, writes,

> As a Guide camping was the highlight. During the war years camp was Spartan, the menu mainly raw vegetables. Activities – no crafts or games but helping on the farm. Only cold water to wash in! Tough maybe, but what a grounding for life.

And finally from Cheshire, May Trill writes,

> To me Guiding has been not so much a programme more a way of life. A Promise made at 7 is like a seed still growing at 83.

And what about the author? She realised early on that Guiding complemented her faith, giving her a code by which to live. Quite simply, the two of them have made her what she is.

Bibliography

Baden-Powell, Agnes and Sir Robert, *How Girls can Help to Build up the Empire* (1912), facsimile edition 1993

Baden-Powell, Heather, *Baden-Powell Family Album* (Alan Sutton, 1986 and 2007)

Forbes, Cynthia, *If it hadn't been for Agnes*, MS of a talk

Hillcourt, William and Olave, Lady Baden-Powell, *Baden-Powell – Two Lives of a Hero* (Heinemann, 1964)

Jeal, Tim, *Baden-Powell* (Hutchinson, 1989)

Kerr, Rose, *The Story of the Girl Guides* (The Girl Guides Association 1932 and 1976)

Liddell, Alix, *The First Fifty Years* (The Girl Guides Association, 1960)

and the following archives

The Baden-Powell family archives

The Girl Guides Ontario Province, Canada

Girlguiding Essex

Girlguiding UK

The Girl Scouts of America

Juliet Gordon Low birthplace

The National Newspaper Library

The Royal Aeronautical Association

The Royal Flying Club, Hendon

The Scout Association

South Georgia Institute

Professor Dame Margaret Turner-Warwick

Index